Experimental Theatre

Other books in this series:

Experimental Painting
Construction · Abstraction · Destruction · Reduction
by Stephen Bann

Experimental Architecture
by Peter Cook

Experimental Cinema
by David Curtis

Experimental Theatre

from Stanislavsky to today

James Roose-Evans

UNIVERSE BOOKS
New York City

For John and Wendy Trewin to whose encouragement and friendship I owe so much—in gratitude

'What a pleasure to hear from you afresh—the wonderful fireworks of a creative mind bombarding the asbestos drop that still seems to confine the passion of the drama to the 19th century. It's cursed with over two thousand years of literal tradition. Now we are listening and looking at either genes or macrocosmic happenings and drama stutters at the task of identifying itself with man's new love affair with the universe. What a task you face, but what an adventure!'

ALWIN NIKOLAIS TO JAMES ROOSE-EVANS

PN
2189
R6

© James Roose-Evans 1970

Published in Great Britain 1970 by
Studio Vista Limited, Blue Star House,
Highgate Hill, London N19
and in the United States of America in 1970
by Universe Books
381 Park Avenue South, New York City, 10016

Library of Congress Catalog Card Number: 72–105962

American SBN 87663–119–7

British SBN 289 79698 9

Set in 11 pt Modern Extended

Printed and bound in Great Britain by
Richard Clay (The Chaucer Press) Ltd
Bungay, Suffolk

Contents

'It is necessary to picture not life itself as it takes place in reality, but as we vaguely feel it in our dreams, our visions, our moments of spiritual uplift. . . .

For the new art new actors are necessary, actors of a new sort with an altogether new technique.'

Constantin Stanislavsky

1 Introduction

To experiment is to make a foray into the unknown—it is something that can be charted only after the event. To be *avant-garde* is truly to be way out in front. Each of the key figures in this book has opened up the possibilities of theatre as an art and for each of them experiment has necessarily implied something very different. For Stanislavsky it meant the importance of the actor, whereas for Craig the actor was practically dispensable, the emphasis being upon the scenic possibilities of theatre. Meyerhold stressed the importance of the director; Appia, the use of light. Brecht, like his master, Piscator, was concerned to explore the didactic nature of the theatre. Artaud, like Stanislavsky, came to believe that theatre should reflect not the everyday reality of naturalism but rather those intimations that are beyond the reach of words. Much that was foreseen by the early pioneers has come to be realized in the American modern dance. The theatre of Alwin Nikolais represents in many ways a synthesis of Artaud's concept of a non-verbal theatre, Craig's idea of moving abstract masses, and the early technical experiments of the Bauhaus.

Of necessity, in a book of this length, much has had to be omitted. A separate book would need to be written about the experiments of dramatists, from the realistic plays of Chekhov to the socially and politically orientated dramas of Shaw and Brecht, and such modern dramatists as Beckett and Pinter who have attempted to write 'about silence, about the things which people do not say' (Virginia Woolf).

This book ends with a chapter on the American scene, simply because the greatest variety and intensity of experimentation today is to be found in the United States. Yet the contemporary figure whose influence would seem to be making the greatest impact both in America and in Europe, is Jerzy Grotowski.

Like Copeau, Grotowski has gone back to the essence of theatre, to the live relationship of actor and audience. His concern is with 'the spectator who has genuine spiritual needs and who really wishes, through confrontation with the performance, to analyse himself'. He is not concerned with theatre as entertainment, as illusion, as magic or as instruction.

By 'analyse' he does not imply an intellectual process so much as a means of 'self-healing' in the Jungian sense. His theatre requires meditation and reflection, seeking communion rather than communication.

The work of Grotowski's Polish Laboratory Theatre, which has influenced the experiments of Peter Brook in England, of Joseph Chaikin and Peter Schumann in New York, raises the whole question of symbolism, the purpose of which is not to increase the quantity of our knowledge and information but to deepen and enrich the quality of life itself, bringing man into communion with those mysterious sources of creativity whereby he can renew himself from within. In an age of outer space, Grotowski invites us to explore the space within. His theatre implies a spiritual view of man, and most recalls the ceremonies of Shamanizing, many of which still exist today.

During the purification ceremonies of the Canadian Eskimo Shaman, the aspirant continually cries out, 'All this because I wish to be seeing!' By gaining control of his own unconscious imagery the Shaman brings into order his own chaotic psyche and that of the community to which he belongs. It is a process of self-healing. The songs and rituals of such a community enable it to master those emotions that might otherwise overwhelm it, enabling each man to understand his own condition more clearly.

Similarly, the Polish Laboratory Theatre takes the myths of its own tradition and by re-experiencing them, strengthens the collective psyche. To this extent its work has its roots as much in Poland as that of The Living Theatre or the Bread and Puppet Theatre have theirs in America.

It is perhaps significant that the Shaman can only reach a small group. In the theatre of today there is an increasingly important part to be played by such cells of activity as The Dancers' Workshop in San Francisco; the Bread and Puppet Theatre and the Open Theatre in New York; the Laboratory Theatre at Wroclaw in Poland, and Stage Two in England.

Such groups are attempting to see theatre not as a sophisticated entertainment, or an intellectual pursuit, but as an experience of life itself. 'There, at the centre, are the artists who really form the consciousness of their time; they respond deeply, intuitively, to what is happening, what has happened and what will happen, and their response is expressed in metaphor, in image and in fable' (John Wain).

2 Stanislavsky's life in art

At the turn of this century Russia was a land of giants. From the 'nineties onwards there was a time of volcanic eruption in the arts, bringing in its wake an entire social, religious and ideological upheaval—the emergence of a new society. A roll-call of that period catches some of the excitement—Tolstoy, Dostoevsky, Chekhov, Gogol, Tchaikovsky, Rimsky-Korsakov, Chaliapin, Diaghilev, Pavlova, Karsavina, Nijinsky, Bakst, Benois, Fokine and, of course, Stanislavsky.

Constantin Stanislavsky (1863–1938) is the great patriarchal figure not only of the Russian theatre but of theatre throughout the Western world. Of all the pioneers he casts the longest shadow. Great as were his achievements as director and actor, however, his most important contribution lay in the light he threw upon the technique of acting. His 'system', based upon the observation of good acting practice, has been developed and adjusted according to the needs of different temperaments and nationalities. It was never intended to be a rigid system: 'Create your own method,' he would say. The Method, as we know it, is merely the result of his system first taught in America by two of his protégés, Michael Chekhov and Richard Boleslavsky, and subsequently adapted to the needs of the American actor by Lee Strasberg. The greatness of Stanislavsky lies as much in his flexibility as in his adherence to the cardinal principle of inner truth on the stage. His legacy was, and remains, the Moscow Art Theatre. Kenneth Tynan, describing the giants at the Maly Theatre playing with a selfless economy and precision reminiscent of a group of chess champions at a tournament, records:

It is the same at the Moscow Art Theatre, ripe in years, robust as oaks, beaming in their beards and their supreme authority, the masters play together as Stanislavsky taught and as they can still teach the world.

The joy of seeing master craftsmen working in unison, with the humane poetry and not just the neurotic trimmings of naturalism, is something I had never known until I saw these perdurable players. This is Stanislavsky without Freud, physiological acting without the psychiatric glosses beloved of so many American 'Method' actors; it has subtlety and absolute inevitability . . . The power and the glory of Soviet theatre resides in its older actors, who are by far the finest I have ever seen . . .

Whatever thread one takes up in the history of twentieth-century drama leads back to Stanislavsky. The most austere figure of contemporary theatre, Jerzy Grotowski, acknowledges his debt to him: 'His persistent study, his systematic renewal of the methods of observation, and his dialectical relationship to his own earlier work make him my personal ideal.' In his thinking Stanislavsky anticipated many of the major developments in theatre. Through all the vicissitudes of fashion, however, he retained his belief in the essential creative power of the actor as the only source of vitality for the theatre.

Stanislavsky felt that the director of a theatre which was to fulfil a 'cultural mission' should have a first-hand and expert knowledge of all the elements of theatre: he should be familiar with it from the actor's, director's, producer's and administrator's points of view. One rarely comes across all these qualities in one person—but they were combined in Vladimir Nemirovich-Danchenko. 'He was that director of whom one could dream. It seems that he had also dreamed of such a theatre as I had imagined and sought a man such as he imagined me to be.'

His meeting with Danchenko in 1896 was to have a profound influence not only on the theatre in Russia but throughout the world. From it sprang one of the most important events in theatrical history. By founding the Moscow Art Theatre both Stanislavsky and Nemirovich-Danchenko were rebelling against the conventional, declamatory style of acting, against a star system which prevented the development of an ensemble style of acting. 'Like all revolutionaries,' wrote Stanislavsky, 'we broke the old and exaggerated the new.'

At the time, Nemirovich-Danchenko was one of the best of the younger Russian dramatists, and was considered to have inherited the mantle of Ostrovsky. He had shared the Griboyedov Prize with Chekhov who had submitted The Seagull. Because it seemed to him that Chekhov's play was immeasurably superior to his own, he declined his half of the prize in favour of his rival. With the founding of the Moscow Art Theatre it was his idea to include The Seagull in the first season, and it was he who suggested that Stanislavsky should direct it. In Anton Chekhov the Moscow Art Theatre found a dramatist whom they were uniquely gifted to interpret. As Stanislavsky said, 'Chekhov gave that inner truth to the stage which served as the foundation for what was later called the Stanislavsky System, which must be approached through Chekhov, or which serves as a bridge to the playing of Chekhov.'

By 1904 the plays of Chekhov, Gorki, Ibsen, Knut Hamsun, Shakespeare, Tolstoy and Maeterlinck, as well as the exceptionally high standard of design, acting and directing, had made the theatre a success. Diaghilev, writing on 'The Originality of the Moscow Art Theatre' in his publication The World of Art, observed that because of its proven success and popularity this company could risk innovations in the theatre which with any less well-established group would have been condemned to ridicule.

In spite of their success, however, Stanislavsky was filled with doubts. He felt that they had become trapped by the very realism they had set out to achieve. Compared with what was happening in the other arts, in the new painting, music and sculpture, the theatre seemed antiquated. It was during this period that he came into contact once again with Vsevolod Meyerhold, a former member of the company, who had created the part of Konstantin in *The Seagull* and had left in order to start up his own group in the provinces. Like Stanislavsky he was seeking something new in art, something more contemporary and modern in spirit.

The difference between the two men lay in the fact that while Stanislavsky strained towards the new without knowing how to realize it, Meyerhold believed that he had already found it but was unable to realize it through lack of means and opportunity. Since the daily rehearsal and performance schedule of a repertory theatre provided no room for experimental laboratory work, Stanislavsky decided to help him. He opened the Theatrical Studio where, with a group of young actors, Meyerhold was to be free to carry out his ideas. The principle of the new studio was that realism and local colour had outlived their usefulness and no longer interested the public. 'The time for the unreal on the stage had arrived. It was necessary to picture not life itself as it takes place in reality, but as we vaguely feel it in our dreams, our visions, our moments of spiritual uplift.'

After a summer in which Meyerhold and his young actors were left to work without interruption, Stanislavsky saw a dress rehearsal of Maeterlinck's *The Death of Tintagels*, and Hauptmann's *Schluck und Jan*. Although there was a great deal that was new, unexpected and often beautiful, Stanislavsky felt that the actors were too young and inexperienced. He was acutely conscious of the gulf between the director's dreams and their realization—since only the actor could fulfil this dream: *For the new art new actors were necessary, actors of a new sort with an altogether new technique*. But there were no such actors in the Studio and Stanislavsky felt that to open it in such an incomplete state would be harmful to its very *raison d'être*: 'A good idea, badly shown, dies for a long time.' It was at this moment that the First Revolution broke and so the opening of the Studio was delayed indefinitely. Stanislavsky had to pay off the actors, close the Studio and spend the next several years paying off its debts. Meyerhold returned to the Moscow Art Theatre to play Konstantin in *The Seagull*, which part he had created in the original production.

Meanwhile Stanislavsky and Nemirovich-Danchenko saw clearly that they had reached a crossroads; that it was necessary to refresh themselves and the company. There seemed no point in remaining in Moscow, not simply because of the revolutionary climate, but because they had no concrete idea of what they might achieve there. The death of their beloved playwright Anton Chekhov, the death of their patron Morozov, the failure of the

Maeterlinck plays, the catastrophic demise of the Studio project, as well as Stanislavsky's own dissatisfaction with himself as an actor, 'and the complete darkness that lay before me, gave me no rest, took away all faith in myself'. In this state of mind he went to spend the summer of 1906 in Finland.

It is at those moments of extreme despair and seeming disintegration in an artist's life that new life is often stirring; when an impasse seems to have been reached a new path is often discovered. So with Stanislavsky in the summer of 1906. 'Sitting on a bench in Finland and examining my artistic past'—was to prove the beginning of what is now known as The Stanislavsky System. In 1906 he enjoyed a world-wide reputation as an actor, director and co-founder of the Moscow Art Theatre. With more than thirty years' experience behind him, he had acquired a vast amount of knowledge about acting technique. But everything was thrown together indiscriminately and in such a form that, in order to make further progress, he had first to analyse his accumulated experience.

The results of his analysis were set out in his two books, *My Life In Art* and *An Actor Prepares* (which David Magarshack more accurately translates as *An Actor's Work on Himself*). He declared,

The basis of my system is formed by the laws of the organic nature of the actor which I have studied thoroughly in practice. Its chief merit is that there is nothing in it I myself invented or have not checked in practice. It is the natural result of experience of the stage over many years . . . Directors explain very cleverly what sort of result they want to get. They tell the actor what he should *not* do, but they do not tell him *how* to achieve the required result.

It is always interesting to trace the first influences upon any great artist, and none more so than Stanislavsky. One of a large and wealthy family, he was educated at home. As a boy he was taught ballet by Yekaterina Sankovskaya, one of the most outstanding ballerinas in Russia. Noted particularly for her strong dramatic talent and her interest in the psychological motivation of the characters she portrayed, she perhaps planted the first seed in the young Constantin. He next came under the influence of Mikhail Shchepkin, the great Russian actor of the first half of the nineteenth century. He was the first in that country to introduce simplicity and life-likeness into a performance, and he taught his pupils to observe the manner in which emotions are expressed in real life. Stanislavsky records how, as a youth, he tried to acquaint himself with everything Shchepkin wrote about dramatic art in his letters to Gogol and other friends. 'Always have nature before

your eyes,' he wrote to a fellow actor: 'enter, so to speak, into the
skin of the rôle you are playing; study well the social background
of the character . . . and don't forget to study the past life of the
character . . . therefore study all classes of society.' He would
repeat over and over to his students, 'It is not important that you
play well or ill; it is important that you play truthfully.'

For the Stanislavskys amateur theatricals were a family pursuit.
As the children grew older and became more experienced so they
would stage whole plays, even operas. One year they decided to
do *The Mikado*. All that winter their home resembled a corner of
Japan, and they even had a troupe of Japanese acrobats, who
were appearing in a circus, to stay with them. Returning from the
office or factory the young actors would put on their Japanese
costumes, wearing them all evening and, during the holidays, all
day as well! Stanislavsky records how they spent one whole day
behaving not as themselves but as the characters in the play. The
girls also practised walking about with their legs tied together as
far as the knee and learned how to use the fan. 'I do not doubt,'
he comments, 'that the work we then accomplished, although it was
temporary and soon forgotten, nevertheless planted certain seeds
of the future in our souls.'

The young Constantin was always studying, observing and
absorbing. When the famous Meiningen Players came to Moscow
he went to every one of their performances, 'not only to look but
to study as well'. Similarly, years later, when he was famous, he
attended every single one of Isadora Duncan's recitals. All his
life he was relentless in his search for knowledge and in his quest for
inner truth on the stage, the truth of feeling and experience.

In his experiments on himself as an actor Stanislavsky displayed
a determination and an objectivity that one can only parallel
with the work of some of the modern dancers such as Martha
Graham, or a teacher like Mathias Alexander. The actor, the
dancer, the singer has to work through his own muscles, his own
body, his own emotions: often there is no one to teach or to guide
him. He is his own instrument. For years, like Graham, like
Alexander, Stanislavsky preached his artistic credo with enthusiasm but without any success. 'A wall rose between me and
the company. For years our relationship was cold.'

As with Copeau when he founded the School of the Vieux-
Colombier, the actors of the Moscow Art Theatre were jealous of
Stanislavsky's work with the young actors. It was only after
several years that his system began to be accepted by the older
actors—at least in part. The danger was, however, that they
learned the terminology but neglected the continuous exercises.
Stanislavsky did not shut his eyes to the fact that his system
required so great a devotion to the art of the stage that only a

few actors were equal to it. In later life he confessed to the many disappointments he had had; although he had worked with hundreds of actors only a few of them had had the will-power and perseverance necessary for 'real art'.

In order to help the young people who came to him he founded the first Studio under the leadership of Sulerjitsky, and entrusted their training to Evgeny Vakhtangov. He bought and presented to the Studio a large plot of land on the shores of the Black Sea, where the young actors built communal buildings, a small hotel, stables, cowsheds, barns. Each actor built his own house which then became his own property, while everyone took part in the communal tasks. It was a Tolstoyan existence. It was to prove an ideal, a way of life and a way of work that would haunt the imagination of other artists at various times. Vera Komisarjevskaya, the sister of Theodore Komisarjevsky, dreamed of such a community of artists; Copeau formed a group of actors and, twice in the career of the Vieux-Colombier, took them away to live and work in the country. His successor, Michel Saint-Denis, did likewise with the Compagnie des Quinze. So did Charles Dullin. So, too, the Group Theatre in America in the 'thirties, The Living Theatre, and Peter Schumann's Bread and Puppet Theatre in the 'sixties. Vera Komisarjevskaya dreamed of a company of actors united by the same understanding of the art of acting. She came to the conclusion that a theatre of ideas needs interpreters who have been brought up on the ideas and methods of that particular theatre. 'Every such theatre must be like a community, following a "master", something like what in the art of painting is called a "school", in which all the disciples carry out freely and enthusiastically the ideas of their leader and are able to work together on the same picture.'

3 The school of realism

The movement towards greater truth on the stage, 'to hold, as 't were, the mirror up to nature', stemmed, however, not from Russia but from Europe, and its first clear definition was provided by Victor Hugo. In 1827 Hugo, then twenty-five, published his famous manifesto in which he declared that life, and life alone, in all its variety was the only model for the stage. The stage should feel free to present any subject and to use any form or style.

'Let us take the hammer to theories and poetic systems,' he pronounced. 'Let us throw down the old plastering that conceals the façade of art. There are neither rules nor models; or, rather, there are no other rules than the general rules of nature which soar above the whole field of art and the special rules which result from the conditions appropriate to the subject of each composition.'

He rejected as unnatural the division of comedy and tragedy, and the classical unities of time, place and action. Although the German playwrights of the *Sturm und Drang* school, fifty years previously, had fought for greater freedom to experiment, Victor Hugo's introduction to *Cromwell* became the most important manifesto of the new realism. His *Hernani*, presented at the Théâtre Français in 1830, created an uproar and was soon followed by the plays of Zola, Ibsen, Strindberg—as well as a play by the Goncourt Brothers who were ardent supporters. As the nineteenth century became increasingly industrialized, its outlook more materialistic and scientific, so the movement towards realism in the theatre gathered momentum. And with the new plays there came the demand for an equal realism in their staging. Although there had been a vogue for illusionist sets in the Italian court theatres of the Renaissance, these had not been used naturalistically as part of the environment to which the characters in the play belonged, but merely as stunning backgrounds before which the actors strutted and exhibited themselves.

The new drama not only paved the way for a new approach to décor but led also to the creation of the director-producer whose task it was to create an overall unity of design and style for the production. One of the first companies to demonstrate the importance of the director was that of the Meiningen Players, founded in 1874 by George II, Duke of Saxe-Meiningen, who designed and directed all the productions, assisted by the actor Ludwig Kronek. Of the various innovations for which the company became famous, that of historical accuracy of costumes and settings was derived from earlier experiments in the English theatre, the work of Kemble, Macready, Madame Vestris and Charles Kean. The latter used to engage antiquarians and scholars to help create 'authentic', historically correct sets. It is also probable that the Duke, who was related to Queen Victoria and often used to visit

London, may have seen the production of Tom Robertson's *Caste* with its very naturalistic set.

The Duke, however, was the first to set his actors within the environment of the décor, thereby breaking up that formality of grouping which was so characteristic of the period, especially on the French stage. He employed steps and rostra to keep the action moving on different levels. He insisted that all gestures be within the period of the play's setting. Above all, he brought to his crowd scenes such detail of characterization as was to astound the rest of the world and to have a profound effect on such directors as Stanislavsky in Russia and Antoine in France.

He demonstrated, as had no one before him, the advantage of visualizing a production in its entirety, thereby giving it a unity of style and interpretation. As an orchestra needs a conductor, so he revealed the need for a theatre ensemble to have a director. It was the Duke of Saxe-Meiningen who inaugurated long rehearsal periods for a production, and his actors would work with the sets, costumes and properties from the very beginning. 'It is always an advantage,' he wrote, 'for an actor to touch a piece of furniture or some object naturally; that enhances the impression of reality.'

Antoine, who founded the Théâtre Libre in Paris in 1887, was to develop this argument. 'We must not be afraid of an abundance of little objects, of a wide variety of props,' he wrote. 'These are the imponderables which create a sense of intimacy and lend authenticity to the environment which the director seeks to re-create . . . Among so many objects . . . the performer's acting becomes more human, more intense, and more alive in attitude and gestures.'

Antoine believed that a set should be designed with its four walls in mind 'without worrying about the fourth wall which will later disappear so as to enable the audience to see what is going on.' It was first necessary to create the environment; it was this that would determine the movements and 'business' of the actors within the given circumstances and physical environment of the play.

Just as Antoine, in his enthusiasm for realism, hung up chunks of real meat in a scene set in a butcher's shop; just as David Belasco in America had real buildings transferred in their entirety on to the stage; so, too, the Moscow Art Theatre was at first obsessed by a passion for historical and realistic detail. But such extremes were a natural phase in the process of experimentation, and gradually Stanislavsky moved away from his early emphasis on external, or photographic, realism and began to search for an inner realism. He realized that the actor had to select those aspects of reality which would serve to create an *impression* of reality. Similarly, although Zola wanted drama to be 'unarranged', presented unequivocally as *une tranche de vie*, authors such as Ibsen, Shaw, Chekhov and Strindberg were aware of the need to select and arrange material.

There seems to be no trace in available records of what happened to the Meiningen Players. One suspects that in the company's very success lay the seeds of its decline. It was an ensemble achieved at the price of autocracy: neither the Duke nor Kronek were concerned with the contribution of the individual actor. Stanislavsky himself, seeing what they had been able to achieve, became at first a despotic director. Faced with amateur, second-rate or inexperienced actors, he admitted a need for the director to dictate the whole production. The amazing detail and inventiveness of his production of *The Seagull* were conceived and written down while on holiday, and then dictated to the company. In the early days of the Moscow Art Theatre, in order to achieve a new style, Stanislavsky was obliged to impose his ideas. Gradually, as he came to realize the need to train new actors, his system was evolved. Where the Meiningen Players, having created a standard of external excellence in production and a brilliance of detail, did not continue to explore and develop, the Moscow Art Theatre was able to grow with the artistic growth of its director.

Although at first the Moscow Art Theatre was to perfect the naturalistic style and to become renowned for its realistic productions of Chekhov, it also experimented with other forms of theatre. Joshua Logan, in his foreword to Sonia Moore's book on Stanislavsky, records his surprise at Stanislavsky's interpretation of *The Marriage of Figaro* by Beaumarchais:

. . . it was done with a racy, intense, farcical spirit which we had not associated with Stanislavsky. It was as broad comedy playing and directing as anything we had ever seen. The high-styled members of the cast in flashing coloured costumes would run, pose, prance, caress, faint, stutter in confusion, and play out all the intricate patterns of the French farce with a kind of controlled frenzy.

Another outstanding memory of Logan's visit to Moscow was Tolstoy's *Resurrection*, directed by Nemirovich-Danchenko. In this the director took full advantage of the revolving stage of the Moscow Art Theatre and a great deal of the effect of the production was visual; André van Gyseghem, in *The Theatre in Soviet Russia 1943*, described it as 'the most revolutionary production in the repertoire'. For it a new character was written into the play, that of Tolstoy, to fill in the gaps, speak the thoughts of the characters, comment on and add a counterpoint to the action. Also in this production the Moscow Art Theatre broke the convention of the picture-frame stage. Katchalov, as Tolstoy, played in the orchestra pit, by the proscenium arch, at the side of the stage, in the auditorium, by the side of characters whose thoughts he spoke, and for one whole scene he spoke alone while the actors on stage said nothing.

Unfortunately, the success of the Moscow Art Theatre with its realistic productions was to dog its reputation for many years. 'There was an opinion extant at that time,' wrote Stanislavsky, 'an opinion which it is impossible to overthrow, that our theatre was a realistic theatre only . . . and yet . . . who was it who was really interested in the quest for and creation of the abstract? But once an idea gets lodged in the mind of the public it is hard to dislodge it.'

It is therefore worth recalling some of Stanislavsky's stylistic experiments. In an early production of Hauptmann's *The Sunken Bell* he broke up the surface of the stage as a challenge to his actors. 'Let them creep, I thought, or sit on stones. Let them leap on the cliffs or climb the trees. Let them descend into the trap and climb back again. This will force them, and myself too, to get used to a new mise-en-scène, and to play in a way that is new to the stage.'

In *The Drama of Life* by Knut Hamsun, Stanislavsky achieved a special effect by the use of shadow play. The tents of the circus booths were made of oiled linen and, by the use of back lighting, the silhouettes of the crowd were outlined. The tents were placed on platforms rising one above the other, so that the entire stage seemed filled with the whirling shadows of people rising and falling on roundabouts. The success of this particular production, so totally unlike the realism of Stanislavsky's Chekhov productions, caused the progressive element in the audience to shout out, 'Death to realism! Down with crickets and mosquitos!' while the more conservative members retorted, 'Shame on the Art Theatre! Down with decadence!'

For Andreyev's *The Life of Man* the stage was covered entirely in black velvet—when Isadora Duncan saw it she said, *'Mon Dieu, c'est une maladie!'*—against which was a set made of rope, suggesting the outline of doors, windows, etc. All the furniture and the costumes of the actors were in black and outlined in rope, the colour of which varied with each act, white, pink and gold. With this particular production it was said that the theatre had discovered new paths in art, but, as Stanislavsky remarked, 'these paths, as is always the way with scenic revolutions in the theatre, did not go any further than the scenery'. It was this production that was to prove a historical turning point in his life, for in spite of its success he did not feel that the actors had moved forward. From that moment on, his work and his attention were devoted almost completely to the study and teaching of inner creativeness. The more disappointed Stanislavsky became in the means of theatrical production, the more he entered into the inner creative work of the actor. In a production of *A Month in the Country* he even attempted to do away with all mise-en-scène and had the actors seated on a bench speaking their inmost thoughts. Ironically, as he observes, 'As the outward side of our productions retreated more and more to the background, so in the other theatres of Moscow and Petrograd more and more interest was displayed in the outer appearances in contra-distinction to the inner contents of the play.'

4 Meyerhold and the Russian avant-garde

Stanislavsky was referring, of course, to the productions of such avant-garde directors as Meyerhold and Taïrov who often cared more about the form than the content of the play. Norris Houghton vividly describes Meyerhold's general approach to a play in an account of a talk given by Meyerhold to his actors at the first rehearsal for a production of three one-act plays by Chekhov, *The Proposal*, *The Bear* and *The Jubilee*.

Two things are essential for a play's production, as I have often told you. First, we must find the thought of the author; then we must reveal that thought in a theatrical form. This form I call a *jeu de théâtre* and around it I shall build the performance . . . In this production I am going to use the technique of the traditional vaudeville as the *jeu*. Let me explain what it is to be. In these three plays of Chekhov I have found that there are thirty-eight times when characters either faint, say they are going to faint, turn pale, clutch their hearts, or call for a glass of water; so I am going to take this idea of fainting and use it as a sort of leit-motif for the performance. Everything will contribute to this *jeu*.

In 1932 both Stanislavsky and Nemirovich-Danchenko were to come out with sharp criticism of formalistic innovators and to defend realism on the stage as the only sound tradition. This accorded with previous announcements condemning 'excessive experiment'. Already, in 1926, they had staged Ostrovsky's *The Burning Heart* as an answer to Meyerhold, affirming the theatre of the actor and of psychological treatment of characters as opposed to the avant-garde treatment of the actor as a puppet.

After the ill-fated Experimental Theatre Studio, Vsevolod Meyerhold was invited to be the director of Vera Komisarjevs-kaya's theatre. Here he was given the opportunity to put into practice all his ideas. For *Hedda Gabler* he removed the proscenium arch and presented an entirely non-realistic production based on the French symbolists' principle of correspondence between moods and colours—each character having his own colour and fixed set of gestures. For Maeterlinck's *Sister Beatrice* in order to bring audience and actors closer, he had the scenery, decorative flats, brought down-stage, leaving only a shallow platform so that the actors resembled figures carved in a bas-relief. Instead of in-dividualizing the crowd, as would have been done at the Moscow Art Theatre, he had groups moving in unison like a medieval frieze. His aim was to convey not the feelings of individual characters but purified 'extracts' of emotion. The actors were trained to speak in a form of recitative limited to three notes and to move in a slow, hieratic style. Often it seemed as though Meyerhold were trying to turn his actors into puppets, reminding one, as Marc Slonim observes, of the French nursery rhyme—
'*Les petites marionettes font, font, font leurs trois petites tours et puis s'en vont.*'

Maeterlinck's *Pelléas et Mélisande* was interpreted by Meyerhold as a fairy tale with settings from a children's book. In *The Little Showbox* by Blok he mixed live actors and marionettes. Each and every production was daring and provocative, moving theatre away from realism: yet they never caught on with the general public. Also, Meyerhold increasingly neglected Vera Komisarjevskaya. Not only the owner of the theatre but also a great actress, she was not content to be treated as a mere marionette, however gifted the puppet-master. He barred her from several of his important productions and, although he went with her to Berlin in 1907 to study the work of Reinhardt, further collaboration between them became impossible. In 1908 he was asked to leave and another innovator, Nikolai Evreinov, replaced him. However, nothing could now save the situation and the theatre closed in 1909. Komisarjevskaya went on tour to America hoping to be able to make enough money to re-open her theatre. She caught pernicious smallpox and died in Russia on 10 February 1910.

For a while Meyerhold went to Minsk to stage plays, using screens instead of sets. He experimented with having the auditorium as well as the stage lit in order to heighten the mood of the spectator and, at the same time, permitting the actor to see exactly what effect he was having. Moving away from sculptural groupings and linear friezes, he became increasingly attracted to the techniques of the circus and the music hall. He came to see mime as superior to words, which were 'but a design on the fabric of movement'. More and more he aimed at breaking down the barrier between stage and audience, building gangways and steps from the stage into the auditorium and having actors moving in the aisles. In The House of Interludes, a theatre where he was able to try out many of his ideas, he had the hall arranged like a tavern with the audience seated at tables drinking while the action took place in their midst, as in a night club.

As a result of the Revolution there were entirely new audiences coming in to the theatre, many of them for the first time, for whom theatre was a new experience. 'Audience participation' was a subject much debated, with those like Meyerhold who were for it, and others who felt that the spectator should remain an observer. Vyachleslav Ivanov, a symbolist poet and playwright, agitated for the return of medieval mysteries in which actor and spectator would be united in a common religious experience. Platon Mikhailovich Kerzhertser, a social theorist, suggested that the audience should not only take an active part in the performance but work in the various other departments of a theatre. Scriabin even advocated what he termed 'preparatory action': in order to be admitted the spectator would have to be initiated, wear special robes, and rehearse his part in a production. There were many, however, who considered that this kind of participation belonged to religious ceremonials, folk festivals and carnivals, political and sports meetings.

In 1911 at the Alexandrinsky Theatre in St Petersburg, Meyerhold was to develop these ideas on a larger and much grander scale. In his production of Molière's *Don Juan,* for instance, he removed the front curtains and the footlights and built a semi-circular proscenium. The stage was lit by huge candelabra and chandeliers, and all the lights in the auditorium were on so that it resembled a vast ballroom. Prompters sat behind Louis Quatorze screens, liveried servants brought on chairs, while little blacka-moors ran to and fro arranging accessories, all to a background of music by Lully. The whole production was regarded as a triumph of 'theatricality' as well as a challenge to the Moscow Art Theatre.

At this period Meyerhold was deeply influenced by the conventions of the Chinese and Japanese theatre. He maintained that attempts to create reality on stage were doomed. He believed that the essence of theatre, as in the Kabuki or in the Kathakali dance theatre of India, lay in the appeal to an audience to use its imagination. This was the principle also of the Globe Theatre and Shakespeare's 'On your imaginary forces work!' Meyerhold's ideas were influenced by Pavlov's Theory of Association which was currently fashionable. He considered that it was the task of the director to work consciously on the known associations of his audience, who know they are being asked to participate, 'The audience is made to see what we want them to see.'

In 1915, in *The Unknown* by Blok in which he employed jugglers and Chinese boys throwing oranges into the audience, there was one scene, typical of his work at this period, in which an astronomer observes a falling star. This was represented by a stage-hand with a lighted torch on the end of a bamboo pole making a circle of flame in the air, and another stage-hand on the opposite side of the stage extinguishing it in a bucket of water.

When the House of Interludes was closed he continued his experiments, under the name of Dr Dappertutto, in various of the workshops that were springing up all over the country. By 1927 there were 24,000 theatre groups in Russia. These were the years of experiment, of studios, workshops and theatre schools. It was almost entirely due to the influence of Meyerhold that the theatre of the revolution became the theatre of the avant-garde. As Marc Slonim points out, in no other country and at no other time were experimentalists given such financial and material opportunities as they were under Lenin, even though he was a conservative in art.

One of the most colourful and idiosyncratic experimenters was

Nikolai Evreinov who succeeded Meyerhold as director of Vera Komisarjevskaya's theatre. In 1908 he published his ideas on theatre in a sensational article in which he claimed that theatre is an organic urge as basic as hunger or sex. From children's games of cops and robbers to military parades, public receptions, religious ceremonies and even the wearing of clothes, consciously or unconsciously, we all play a part, whether we are conforming to certain rules of etiquette or to what is expected of us in our particular profession or social status. Of course, granted such a premise, the theatre of naturalism is meaningless. The true aim of theatre, he argued, was 'theatricalization of life'. According to Evreinov the whole evolution of the European theatre towards realism was a ghastly mistake. Like Meyerhold, Taïrov and Vakhtangov, he believed the theatre should not attempt to make audiences forget they are watching a performance.

He set out, therefore, to revive the great theatrical spectacles of the past. At the Ancient Theatre in St Petersburg he revived medieval miracle plays and sixteenth-century farces. Typical of his productions was Adam de la Halle's *Robin and Marion*, a thirteenth-century pastorale in which he had the stage transformed to resemble a castle hall filled with knights, ladies, servants, minstrels—the audience of the play's period. The players were seen arriving, setting up their stage, unpacking their props, disclosing all the tricks of their trade.

The second season of the Ancient Theatre, 1911–12, was devoted to seventeenth-century playwrights: Calderón, Lope de Vega, Tirso de Molina. The stage usually represented the square of a Spanish town with a background of mountains. Evreinov laid great stress on the visual side of a production. His belief that 'words play but a subordinate rôle on the stage and we hear more with the eyes than the ears' was in sympathy with Meyerhold's conviction of the superiority of mime.

In 1920 he staged in Petrograd *The Storming of the Winter Palace*, reproducing the highlights of the Bolshevik uprising. Eight thousand people took part in the show, an orchestra of 500 played revolutionary songs, while a real blast from the warship Aurora, anchored on the Neva River, added to the theatricality of the occasion. In the apotheosis he had a Tree of Freedom around which all the nations were united in brotherly celebration while the soldiers of the Red Army exchanged their rifles for sickles and hammers. Evreinov was obviously inspired, as Marc Slonim observes, by the great festivals of the French Revolution. Such open-air demonstrations reflected the people's desire for monumental and popular spectacles.

It was in 1920 that Meyerhold began to develop his theory of bio-mechanics, a form of training aimed at developing actors who would be part athletes, part acrobats, part animated machines. Bio-mechanics was a gymnastic based upon:

Preparation for an action—pause—
the action itself—pause—
and its corresponding re-action.

Its aim was to discipline both the emotional and muscular response of the actor. As with a dancer, so every movement or gesture made on stage would be calculated, controlled and never spontaneous. The actor was taught to use the space around him as well as to relate in spatial terms to his fellow actors and the objects around him. Just as Alwin Nikolais demands from his dancers motion rather than emotion, so Meyerhold demanded from his actors the vigorous elimination of all human feeling and the creation of an order based upon mechanical laws, the actor was to function as a machine—a somersault, salto-mortale, or head-spring, would suffice to convey certain states of emotion.

In 1921 he began to train a company of actors according to this system of bio-mechanics. The company gave its first performance in April 1922 in *The Magnificent Cuckold* by Crommelynck, a comedy about a miller who, in an attempt to discover his wife's lover, gets all the men in the villiage to pass through her bedroom. For this production Meyerhold stripped the stage bare, removing the front curtain, borders, tormentors and backdrops. In the centre of this space stood a vertical construction suggestive of a mill, divided into various horizontal levels linked by staircases and gangways. This made it possible for a large number of scenes to be played without a break. There were also wheels, rolling discs, windmill sails, a trapeze, a bridge and ramps. On this constructivist set the actors, without make-up and in full light, dressed only in the light blue overalls of mechanics, ran, jumped and swung like acrobats in a gymnasium. Instead of 'true emotion' they presented a variety of athletic exercises and movements, performed to the accompaniment of a jazz orchestra. Meyerhold's theory was that the truth of human relationships and behaviour is best expressed not by words but by gestures, steps, attitudes and poses.

In subsequent productions, like a ring-master, he put his actors through their paces; like a puppet-master he manipulated his marionettes in space. He used mobile constructions, moving walls, pivoting screens, as well as a revolving stage divided into concentric rings each of which could move independently. He aimed at creating a continuity on stage comparable to the cinema. Also, as Piscator and Jean-Louis Barrault were to do later, he used film in his productions. For the next seventeen years Meyerhold continued experimenting and each of his productions was a subject for debate and controversy. In *Terelkin's Death* by Sukhovo-Kobylin, against an abstract décor of geometric forms, his actors swung across the stage on ropes, juggled and struggled with objects that exploded or leaped into the air! In *Earth on its Hindlegs* by Marcel Martinet, the actors roared across the stage on motor-bikes, pedalled on bicycles, dragged on heavy cannons; and at one point a regiment of soldiers marched across the stage! In 1931 Charles Dullin, a contemporary of Jacques Copeau, referred to Meyerhold as 'a creator of forms, a poet of the theatre, who writes with gestures, rhythms, and a theatrical language invented for his needs'. People flocked from all over Russia and from every part of the world to see his productions and to learn his theory of bio-mechanics.

His most controversial and last great production was Gogol's *The Government Inspector*, staged in 1926. He transposed the text and altered the plot, moving the action from a small town to Moscow, turning the Mayor into a General, and so on. There was a semi-circular-shaped set, like the inside of a drum, in which were fifteen doors. The main action took place on a sloping platform which emerged out of the darkness for each scene. In the scene where the officials arrive to bribe Kheslakov secretly, Meyerhold achieved one of his most startling effects. Suddenly, all the doors in the circular wall opened and in each appeared an official offering money. At the end, as the General was carried off in a strait-jacket on a stretcher, a white curtain was lowered, announcing in gold letters the arrival of the real Inspector General. When it was raised, instead of the live actors there were painted dummies arranged like a tableau of the final scene.

From 1928–53, however, the era of Stalin, experiment in art was banned; Meyerhold's powerful friends in the Party grew fewer, and between 1932–4 he was constantly reproached for his 'inimical attitude towards socialist realism'. Although he continued to do some outstanding productions, his theatre began to decline as the actors, rebelling against his autocratic methods, left his company. He tried hard to resist the Party's demand for ideological plays. In January 1932 *Pravda* led an all-out attack on experiment in the arts as a form of decadence. The political trials which had eliminated all Stalin's enemies were now extended to the arts: Meyerhold was denounced as an enemy of socialist realism and politically dangerous. In January 1938 his theatre was closed and he found himself unemployed, branded as an enemy of the State. Only Stanislavsky had the courage to offer him a job with the Moscow Art Theatre Studio but Stanislavsky died that same year.

In June 1939 Meyerhold was present at the All-Union Convention of Theatre Directors, intended by the Party as a public display of submission. He delivered an impassioned speech, declaring that what was happening in the theatre had nothing whatsoever to do with art. With great courage he defended the right of the creative artist to experiment, and denounced the uniformity that was being imposed upon the arts.

Three days later he was arrested and deported to a concentration camp in the Arctic. Shortly after his arrest his wife, the actress Zinaida Raikh, was found assassinated, with her throat cut, her face disfigured and knife wounds all over her body. Whether Meyerhold died in exile or committed suicide is not known.

5 Taïrov and the synthetic theatre

To Alexander Taïrov, as to many of his contemporaries, the actors of the Meyerhold Theatre were mere puppets in the hands of their director. At the same time, however, he considered that the actors of the Moscow Art Theatre were too dominated by the author. Of the school of naturalism he wrote scathingly, 'Little by little the theatre has turned into an experimental laboratory for psychopathological research . . . the naturalistic theatre suffers from a dysentry of formlessness.'

Taïrov believed that theatre was an art in itself and so he sought to train a company of master actors who would be capable of improvising upon an idea in the tradition of the Commedia dell' Arte and developing it before an audience. He believed in what he called 'the synthetic theatre', incorporating in one company all the talents of ballet, opera, circus, music-hall and drama.

Like Meyerhold he insisted upon the spectator's being aware that he was in a theatre. Similarly, he stressed the importance of gesture and movement, although he considered that Meyerhold imposed these arbitrarily from outside. Believing that the actor should be trained to create them from within himself, Taïrov always insisted that the main creator in the theatre is the master-actor.

For him the future of the theatre lay not only in a synthesis of all the arts but in complex machinery which would serve as an extension to the actor's craft. Influenced by Craig and Appia, he used space on the stage to create dynamic and spatial relationships, assisted by an imaginative use of lighting (based upon the theories of Appia), and the choreographed movement of actors. He consistently broke up the flat surface of the stage—'the stage is the keyboard of the actor'—and used a variety of levels, ramps, stairways and abstract shapes. He would discuss the distance between levels in musical terms— according to the kind of movement required—speaking of intervals of $\frac{1}{4}$ or $\frac{1}{8}$ time, etc. His critics accused him of being more concerned with beauty than with intellectual content. Marc Slonim records that in the 'twenties the public went to his theatre as one goes to the ballet. Critics would write of certain productions, 'Alisa Koonen danced beautifully through her rôle', or, 'Tseretelli's designs had delightful variations in a minor key'.

Like Appia he believed in music as the underlying principle, and often compared his actors to musical instruments and himself to a conductor: when staging Oscar Wilde's *Salome* he would refer to the contra-bass of the soldiers, the flute of the young Syrian, the oboe of Salome, etc. He was often accused of paying more attention to the appearance of his actors than to their talent. When asked what kind of actor he hoped to produce he would reply by quoting the requirements of the classical Hindu theatre: 'Freshness, beauty, pleasant face, red mouth, good teeth, a neck round as a bracelet, arms of handsome form, gracious stature, powerful hips, charm, dignity, nobility, pride—without speaking of genius!' Like Grotowski in Poland today, he considered that actors should begin their training at the age of seven, as in the ballet. In his own school the pupils (known as 'The Jumping Jacks') had to learn fencing, acrobatics, juggling, clowning, as well as various forms of movement and dance. He insisted that the actor's movement is more important than his diction, although both had to conform to strict rules of rhythm and dynamics.

In 1899 Adolphe Appia had published his most important work, *Die Musik und die Inszenierung*, in which, among many reforms, he demanded for singers 'a musical gymnastic' which would enable them to coordinate musical and bodily rhythm. Appia related everything to the concepts of Time and Space and, from 1906 onwards, worked with Jaques-Dalcroze, the originator of eurhythmics, in his academy at Hellerau. What later became known as music-visualization was also developed in America by Ruth St Denis, Ted Shawn, and Doris Humphrey.

Under Taïrov rhythm became a distinctive feature at the Kamerny Theatre; for him also music was the purest of the arts, and he endeavoured to make his productions approach music as far as possible. Dialogue would be intoned, chanted, phrased and, in addition, a musical score was composed for each production. Where Meyerhold's theatre was often as raucous as a circus ring, that of Taïrov resembled a mixture of opera and ballet. He foresaw a time when the actor would so master rhythm that he would be able to execute a performance not merely rhythmically but a-rhythmically. He foresaw the use of off-beat movement and a-tonal sound creating new possibilities in theatre. In many of his ideas he was to anticipate the discoveries of modern dance.

Taïrov, like Meyerhold of Jewish extraction, was a cosmopolitan. His theatre, the Kamerny, was a chamber theatre for connoisseurs. With greater patience than Meyerhold he proved the better teacher, while his diplomacy steered him through many political intrigues. But even he was not to escape the machinations of the Party entirely. In 1929 Stalin described the Kamerny as 'deeply bourgeois and alien to our culture', saying recent plays there were 'trash'. Taïrov's desire to continue his experiments with style and form was constantly in conflict with the growing demand to present ideological and propaganda plays. Because of his flexibility and tact, as well as a use of fashionable terminology which enabled him to put the label of 'socialist realism' on completely different, and often conflicting, plays and productions, he did succeed in surviving through the 'thirties. Of all the theatres of the 'twenties the Kamerny had the longest life, but it was bought at the price of sacrifice and compromise.

In 1946 he staged his last production—Chekhov's *The Seagull*. It was said in Moscow that Chekhov's seagull had become Taïrov's swansong. The play was given a concert performance against black drapes and all the actors wore black. Taïrov inserted discussions about naturalism and other trends in the theatre, while Konstantin's search for new forms sounded very much like an attack on the drabness of socialist realism. It was the same year in which Zhdanov and the Party Central Committee condemned all formalism and experimentation in literature and the arts. In 1949 the Kamerny was closed and in 1950 Taïrov died.

6 Vakhtangov's achievement

If Taïrov rejected the theories of both Meyerhold and Stanislavsky, it was Evgeny Vakhtangov's unique achievement to fuse the contributions of these two great directors and thereby point the way to a richer and more varied form of theatre. 'For Meyerhold,' wrote Vakhtangov [whom he called 'dear, beloved master'], 'a performance is theatrical when the spectator does not forget for a second that he is in a theatre, and is conscious all the time of the actor as a craftsman. Stanislavsky [to whom Vakhtangov once wrote, 'I thank life for the opportunity of knowing you . . . I do not know . . . anyone superior to you'] demands the opposite: that the spectator become oblivious to the fact that he is in a theatre and that he be immersed in the atmosphere in which the protagonists of the play exist.'

What made the productions of Vakhtangov unique was precisely the fusion of psychological truth with a greater awareness of theatricality. 'Realism does not take everything from life,' he wrote, 'but only what it needs for the reproduction of a given scene . . . the form must be created by one's fantasy. That is why I call it fantastic realism. The means must be theatrical.'

As a young man Vakhtangov became extremely interested in the work of Meyerhold. 'Each of his productions,' he wrote in his diary, 'is a new theatre. Every one of them would have a whole new direction.' However, he also thought that Meyerhold acted merely from a desire to destroy the old, and this led him to impose upon a play a form that was often alien to its content.

Evgeny Vakhtangov, who was Stanislavsky's favourite, and greatest pupil, studied first under Nemirovich-Danchenko and then, in 1911, was accepted into the Moscow Art Theatre company where he played over fifty rôles. He believed completely in the teachings of Stanislavsky and soon became his assistant. When Stanislavsky formed the First Studio he entrusted to him the training of the young actors. He criticized Vakhtangov's first production in which he allowed the actors to perform for themselves, what he called 'trance acting', rather than for the audience. Indeed, in these first years, Vakhtangov was inclined to take his master's theories too far. For instance, in 1918 when directing *Rosmersholm*, he insisted that the actors should not only think *about* the character they were playing, but *as* the character. 'An actor must live and think as the character,' he declared. Whereas Stanislavsky, who was continually revising his system, considered that the actor should not lose himself in the part.

Vakhtangov's was essentially a poetic approach to theatre without the preciousness or over-romanticism of Taïrov, and he remained, although of the younger generation, alien to the technological devices exploited by other avant-garde directors. In his production of Strindberg's *Eric XIV* which, with Michael Chekhov in the lead, created a furore in Berlin in 1922, he interpreted the whole play through the diseased mind of the mad king. In the throne room the gold ornaments were rusted and the columns bent. There were labyrinths of stairs and passageways, together with a use of wrong perspective, suggestive of the twisted demented turnings of the king's mind. The courtiers were portrayed as 'the dead souls' of the aristocracy and dressed as puppets or ghosts, while the common people were treated realistically.

One of his most famous productions was *The Dybbuk* for the Habima Theatre Studio in Moscow. Without forgetting Stanislavsky's principles of inner truth he managed to forge a grotesque style that laid bare the atmosphere of fear and superstition in the ghetto which succeeds in destroying the young lovers. Sonia Moore describes how, wrapped in a great coat with a hot-water bottle at his side, he would rehearse through the long, cold nights, stopping only to swallow some bicarbonate of soda which helped to ease the pain of the cancer in his side. During this period, although he was gravely ill, he was also directing at his own studio as well as performing in the evenings. Mrs Moore describes how he would seek a different theatrical rhythm for each character, not imposed from without but discovered from within each actor. 'Forget the superfluous imitation of life,' he would say, 'Theatre has its own realism, its own truth. This truth is in the truth of experience and emotions which are expressed on the stage with the help of imagination and theatrical means.'

When *The Dybbuk* opened on 31 January 1922, the critics were full of praise: 'Every gesture, every intonation, every step, every pose and acting detail is brought to such technical perfection that one can hardly imagine anything superior.' Tyrone Guthrie, in his autobiography *A Life in the Theatre*, describes the production as the most exciting he had ever seen.

It is still, after more than forty years, in its rejection of naturalism, its use of symbolism and ritual, its choreography, its musical approach, more 'advanced', more assured and more economical than the work of any director which I have since encountered . . . Vakhtangov, who set the impress of his style on all Habima's earlier work, was a genius.

His last production—he died in May 1922—was Carlo Gozzi's *Turandot*. At the first rehearsal he announced, 'Our work is senseless if there is no holiday mood, if there is nothing to carry the spectators away. Let us carry them away with our youth, laughter and improvisation.' Sonia Moore records how the actors worked on every word, gesture and intonation until it seemed absolutely spontaneous, *as if* improvised. Actors would compete with one another in invention. A scarf would become a beard; a lampshade, an emperor's hat; a towel, a turban; a shawl, a dress, and so on.

Rehearsals would start just after 11 p.m. when Vakhtangov's own performance had ended, and continue until eight the next morning. His demands for discipline were so severe that actors were actually afraid of him. They knew when he had arrived by the sudden silence in the Studio. He could bring actors to elation by his praise, and reduce them to tears with his keen criticism.

Mortally ill, he demanded joy, infectious gaiety from his cast. 'Actors must have joy in their hearts from the feeling of the stage. Without this, theatre is a layman's pastime.' He knew that he had not long to live and yet he would sometimes cancel in a moment what had been achieved during long nights. 'Never stop searching,' he would say, 'and cherish the form which discloses the inner content.' Continually searching for truth and force, he made each rehearsal new. 'Art is search, not final form. If what an actor finds is good, it will be easy to find something better. Even after the opening of the play the rôle should grow.'

On 27 February a dress rehearsal was held especially for Stanislavsky, Nemirovich-Danchenko, and the actors and students of the Moscow Art Theatre. Vakhtangov himself was at home, dying. 'At the first intermission Stanislavsky telephoned to Vakhtangov, and at the second break he hired a sleigh and went to his home. He gave instructions that the performance was not to continue until his return. "I wanted the actors to live truthfully, really cry and laugh," said Vakhtangov. "Do you believe in them?" "Your success is brilliant," Stanislavsky replied; he then returned to the theatre and the performance continued. At the end Stanislavsky said to the actors, "In the twenty-three years of the Moscow Art Theatre's existence there have been few triumphs such as this one. You have found what many theatres have sought in vain for a long time."' (Sonia Moore.)

At the beginning of *Turandot* the actors appear before the front curtain, wearing their ordinary clothes, and tell the audience what they are going to see. The curtain rises and, to a waltz tune, they all dress up in the bits and pieces they find lying about on the stage, converting rags to riches by their imaginative use of them. Stage-hands then come on, dressed in dark blue kimonos and caps and, to the accompaniment of the lilting waltz, set the stage. Scenery descends from the flies, counter-weighted with gaily-coloured sandbags; as these soar into the air, doors and windows, pillars and arches glide smoothly on. So the play begins.

The production exploded on that dark night in the Moscow of 1922 like a brilliant display of fireworks. Those were the days of poverty, hardship and extreme cold (in Moscow) when everything was scarce—food, materials, warmth. Yet out of this very lack Vakhtangov, with a Franciscan gaiety and lightness of spirit, created an experience of joy.

7 Craig and Appia—visionaries

'As I write, it is not easy to refrain from singing—the moment is the most lovely, the most hallowed in all my life—for in a few minutes I shall have given birth to that which has for a long while been preparing far back before I was born, and all during my life, and now I am the one selected to this honour and am amongst the creators.'

Such words might the Virgin Mary have written to her cousin Elisabeth when expecting the birth of her child, the promised Messiah. They are, however, from a letter by Gordon Craig to his friend, the composer Martin Shaw, and are but a prelude to even more extraordinary language which reads like Nietzsche—in which Craig describes his vision of the Theatre of the Future.

The place is without form—one vast square of empty space is before us —all is still—no sound is heard—no movement is seen . . . Nothing is before us—

And from that nothing shall come life—even as we watch, in the very centre of that void a single atom seems to stir—to rise—it ascends like the awakening of a thought in a dream—

No light plays round it, no angles are to be seen, no shadows are visible—only the slow deliberate inexorable ascension of a single form— near it, yet further back, a second and a third atom seems to have come into a half existence— . . .

. . . and while they grow the first atom seems to be disappearing—a fourth, a fifth, a sixth, and seventh . . . slowly shapes continue to rise in endless numbers—to rise and fall while still the folds unfold and close, mounting one higher than another, others falling until there stand before us vast columns of shapes, all single yet all united—none resting
Until
like a dew it settles—no more—enough.
And may my love beginning, have no end.

Craig dreamed of a theatre that would appeal to the emotions through movement alone. There was to be no play or plot, but simply the correlated movements of sound, light and moving masses. The audience would have a kinetic experience. The Bauhaus in the 'twenties was to experiment along similar lines with plays whose 'plots' consisted of nothing more than the pure movement of forms, colour and light.

Influenced by certain illustrations in Serlio's *Five Books of Architecture*, Craig began to have ideas for a machine, rather like an organ, which would operate great cubes, such as he had once seen in Fingal's Cave, causing them to rise or fall at any speed while, from above, similar cubes would descend and ascend. Upon these moving cubes, combined with his famous screens, light would play continually.

And the actors? He wanted to remove them: 'The actor is for me only an insuperable difficulty and an expense.' If actors were to be

C

used then they 'must cease to speak and must *move* only, if they want to restore the art to its old place. Acting is Action—and Dance the poetry of Action.'

Craig's small book *The Art of the Theatre* caused him to become the spokesman, prophet and leader of the revolution against realism. He protested that the theatre had become overburdened with words, its origins being in dance and mime. He defined the good dramatist as one who knows that the eye is more swiftly and powerfully appealed to than any other sense, and in *Towards a New Theatre* he quotes the derivation of the word theatre from the Greek (θέατρον) meaning a place for *seeing* shows.

It was after seeing puppets used by the German director Jessner that Craig conceived the idea of doing away with actors altogether and substituting what he called 'über-marionettes'. The Bauhaus, which set out to employ modern science and technology for artistic ends, was also to experiment with 'plays' in which pieces of machinery or sculpture would whizz or glide across the stage; while actors were dressed to look like robots. Of course a theatre such as Craig conceived of would cost millions of pounds, robots, elaborate machinery and complex lighting being the means by which the director would realize his abstract visions. But is a theatre without actors any more theatre? Does it not then become kinetic art?

'To save the theatre we must destroy it,' wrote Craig. 'We shall build the Theatre of the Future . . . while we are about it, let us measure for an art which will exceed in stature all other arts, an art which says less yet shows more than all. . .

'I prophesy that a new religion will be found contained in it. That religion will preach no more, but it will reveal. It will not show us the definite images which the painter and the sculptor show us. It will unveil thoughts to our eyes, silently—by movement—in visions.'

Norman Marshall records how in his old age Craig admitted that the theatre of which he dreamed was still to come. 'I once said that there are just two kinds of theatre, the old theatre of my master, Henry Irving, and its successor which I once called the theatre of tomorrow. I have changed my ideas. The old theatre has been effectively destroyed. In its place we have a new kind of theatre which is infinitely better but is, in fact, no more than a re-edit of the old model, brought up to date, streamlined and improved. The *real* theatre, the theatre which is an art in its own right like music and architecture, is yet to be discovered and may not come for several generations.'

Craig as a person would seem to have been too paranoiac, irresponsible and immature to carry the weight of his own genius. His fame rests less on his actual work in the theatre than on his writings and designs. Even here his head was in the clouds for, as Lee Simonson has demonstrated, his designs for the theatre were often totally impractical because of his complete disregard for the principle of relativity. Scenic design is governed by the relation between the unchangeable size of the human figure and the height of the set, which in turn is governed by the height of the proscenium arch. A Craig drawing of a six-foot figure is very impressive because of the relation of the figure to the soaring lines of the arch; but when the height of the arch is reduced to twenty feet—which is about as high as it could be in a present-day theatre—the figure of the actor still remains six feet high, with the result that the size of the arch in relation to the figure standing beneath it is no longer particularly impressive.

Craig's famous screens, his Thousand Scenes in One, are an example of his infectious, yet impractical, ideas. In place of painted scenery he visualized scenery made of screens with two-way hinges, which could be composed in any shape and made in any size, and lit in any colour, according to the mood of the scene. The Abbey Theatre in Dublin was the first to use Craig's screens. W. B. Yeats was a great admirer and it was for him that Craig made a miniature set of them which he used to have before him while writing his plays—the different arrangements providing him with all the backgrounds that he required.

It was after reading Craig's article on 'The Artists of the Theatre of the Future' that Stanislavsky invited him to Moscow to design and direct *Hamlet*. For this production Craig decided to use his screens. At first he wanted them built of metal but, as Stanislavsky dryly comments, the sheer weight would have necessitated rebuilding the entire theatre and installing hydraulic machinery! The technicians of the Moscow Art Theatre workshops experimented for many months with various metals, wood, even cork; all were too heavy. 'At each appointed cue,' Craig announced, 'a single or double leaf of my screens moves—turns and advances —recedes—folds and unfolds.' But he had no idea how 'those terrible and dangerous walls'—as Stanislavsky describes them— were to be operated. Eventually the screens were made of timber frames and canvas.

With endless patience—the entire production took two years to prepare—Stanislavsky rehearsed the stage-hands so that the screens should seem to move of their own accord. Then, only one hour before the first performance, when Stanislavsky was sitting in the auditorium, having rehearsed the scene-shifters for the last time and sent them off to have a tea-break, suddenly one of the screens began to topple sideways. It fell on to the next screen and then, one after the other like a house of cards collapsing, the whole set crashed to the stage. There was the sound of canvas ripping, timber snapping, and a mass of broken and torn screens lay heaped on the stage. The audience was already entering. The front curtain was lowered while the stage-hands endeavoured to salvage the wreck. Instead of the screens being moved in full view of the audience, as Craig had intended, the curtains had to be closed for every scene change.

Although Craig was an able craftsman, draughtsman and a brilliant artist, none the less there was in his life and work a basic lack of discipline. He spilled over in too many directions, failing to relate to simple practical realities; because of this the School of Theatre foundered within a few months and not because of the outbreak of war as is sometimes claimed. He was so filled with the general concept of a school that he failed completely to consider the practical details of organization needed to realize his scheme. If, however, many of his ideas seemed impractical at the time, they were still to have a profound influence upon succeeding generations of designers. Josef Svoboda, Robert Edmond Jones, Norman Bel-Geddes, Wieland Wagner, Isamu Noguchi and many others, benefiting by modern technological advances, have been able to give form to many of his ideas. When Isamu Noguchi designed *King Lear* for John Gielgud in 1955 not one critic recognized that his huge screens, gliding about the stage as though of their own volition, were a superb realization of Craig's concept of mobile screens. 'Instead,' Noguchi relates, 'I was deluged with an avalanche of abuse from the press.'

It was Craig's cardinal belief that all great plays have an imaginative décor of their own. When designing Ibsen's *Rosmersholm* for Duse he created not a drawing-room but a dark, greeny-blue space with an opening at the back looking out to a misty distance. In the programme he included a note to explain the idea behind his design.

Ibsen's marked detestation of Realism is nowhere more apparent than in the two plays of *Rosmersholm* and *Ghosts*. The words are the words of actuality but the drift of the words something beyond this. There is the powerful impression of unseen forces closing in upon the place: we hear continually the long drawn-out note of the horn of death . . .

Therefore those who prepare to serve Ibsen, to help in the setting forth of his play, must come to the work in no photographic mood, all must approach as artists . . . Realism is only Exposure whereas Art is Revelation; and therefore in the mounting of this play I have tried to avoid all Realism . . .

Let our common sense be left in the cloak-room with our umbrellas and hats. We need here our finer senses only, the living part of us. We are in Rosmersholm, a house of shadows.

. . . the birth of the new Theatre, and its new Art, has begun.

If, however, many of Craig's later designs became too grandiose to be successfully translated, it is interesting to observe, as Norman Marshall points out in *The Producer and the Play*, that in his early days Craig worked in inadequate halls and with limited resources. His very first opportunity to put some of his ideas into practice came with a production of *Dido and Aeneas*; this he designed and directed for the Purcell Operatic Society which was founded in Hampstead by his friend Martin Shaw, who rehearsed and trained the singers. The production was presented at the Hampstead Conservatoire of Music (later to become the Embassy Theatre) in 1900. To W. B. Yeats who was present it seemed like the dawn of something great—'the only good scenery I ever saw'.

In staging his first production Craig had learned much from the articles and lectures of Hubert von Herkomer, who had a school and theatre at Bushey in Hertfordshire where he wrote his own plays, composed incidental music for concealed orchestra and, with his pupils, acted, danced and sang. Herkomer used effects of misty glens, sunrises, moonlit scenes, waterfalls, etc., all achieved by the use of gauzes and electric light as well as side lighting. Many theatre people went to pick up ideas and Craig was taken by his mother, Ellen Terry.

In 1901 Craig worked again with Martin Shaw on *The Masque of Love* which was presented at the Coronet Theatre. For this he used three walls of light grey canvas and a grey stage cloth. The costumes were black and white with occasional touches of colour. This grey box was filled with pools of coloured light in and out of which moved white-frocked children.

His next production, in 1902, was *Acis and Galatea* at the Penley's Theatre. It is important to stress that for these productions he had little or no money to spend. The singers of the Purcell Operatic Society were gifted amateurs, and neither Craig nor Shaw received any payment for many months' work: everything had to be done on a shoe-string budget. For this new production Craig spent hours rummaging through wholesale houses in the City in search of cheap materials. He found masses of upholsterer's webbing (the kind used for supporting sofa springs), and with this he constructed a huge white tent through the lattices of which light could shine. The costumes were made from yards of ribbon which, as the actors moved in and out of the slits in the tent, floated out behind them.

In spite of the success and importance of each of these productions, the Purcell Operatic Society had to close. Brokers' men arrived at the theatre on the last night, while Ellen Terry, as so often, was left to pay the bills. 'I send cheques to pay *half* the amount of five *pressing* bills you tell me about—"Old bills", you say! Why, I have been paying your "old bills" these ten years!'

Among those who saw *Acis and Galatea* was Laurence Housman who wrote to Craig inviting him to design and direct a nativity play he had written, called *Bethlehem*. The play had music by Joseph Moorat who was prepared to finance a modest production. For it Craig created one of his most evocative effects. When the curtains opened the audience saw an indigo night in which stars were twinkling; in the centre sat the shepherds in a sheepfold full of sleeping sheep. Edward Craig, in his excellent account of the life of his father, tells us that the scene was created by the use of a few sheep hurdles placed in an irregular rectangle; the stars were crystals, taken from an old chandelier, which, suspended at different heights on black cobbler's thread against an indigo back-cloth, sparkled every now and then as they caught the light. The 'sheep' were simply sacks filled with wool, with two sections on the top of each tied off to suggest the ears.

Gordon Craig's most memorable and perhaps best known designs were those for the Moscow Art Theatre's production of *Hamlet*. In the first scene the stage, with its towering screens, seemed full of mysterious corners, passages, deep shadows, shafts of moonlight, the passing of sentries. Strange unfathomable underground sounds, the howling of the wind and distant cries could be heard. From among the grey screens there emerged the ghost, scarcely visible in his grey costume against the grey walls, his long cloak sliding behind him. Suddenly the ghost, caught in a shaft of light, startles the guards but at once fades into one of the apertures in the screens and disappears. The scene of Hamlet's meeting with his father's spirit was placed high up on the battlements against a reddening sky so that the light, shining through the diaphanous material of the ghost's cloak, made him seem about to dissolve with the approach of dawn.

For the Court scene Craig covered the screens with gilt paper, the kind usually used for Christmas decorations. The King and Queen sat on a high throne, wearing gold costumes, while from their shoulders there stretched an enormous gold cloak covering the entire stage. In the cloak were holes through which appeared the heads of the courtiers. The scene was dimly lit so that the gold glimmered against the surrounding darkness.

Thus the artist in the grip of forces stronger than himself, a man caught up in an archetypal dream, of whom Bernard Shaw has said:

If ever there was a spoilt child in artistic Europe, that child was Gordon Craig. The doors of the theatre were wider open to him than to anyone else. He had only to come in as others did, and do his job, and know his place, and accept the theatre with all its desperate vicissitudes, and inadequacies, and impossibilities, as the rest of us did, and the way would have been clear for all the talent he possessed.

The use of darkness, of shadow as a counterpoint to light, combined with architectural masses, was not original to Craig. Indeed, many of his ideas had already been anticipated by the Swiss Adolphe Appia who, in 1891, had published a small pamphlet, *Staging Wagnerian Drama*, which included a complete scenario of *The Ring*. In 1895 he wrote his most important work, *Die Musik und die Inszenierung*, in which he set out in detail his proposed reforms for the revival of scenic art. It was in this book that he advocated a theatre of atmosphere rather than of appearances, remarking that in *Siegfried* 'we need not try to represent a forest; what we must give the spectator is man in the atmosphere of a forest'. Although Irving and the Duke of Saxe-Meiningen were the first to use shadows on stage, Appia was the first to work out a complete theory of stage lighting based on the possibilities of moving lights upon simple, non-representational sets painted a neutral colour. As Lee Simonson remarks in *The Stage is Set*, 'the first hundred and twenty pages of Appia's volume are nothing less than the text-book of modern stagecraft.' It was Appia who first demonstrated the necessity of visualizing the mood and the atmosphere of a play; the importance of suggestion completed in the imagination of the spectator; the effectiveness of an actor stabbed by a spotlight in a great dim space; the significance of a 'space-stage'; and the more abstract forms of scenic art. He foresaw not only the possibility of spot-lighting but also of projected scenery, something Craig had never imagined.

Light was to Appia the supreme scene painter; light alone defined and revealed. The very quality of our emotional response can, as we now know, be established by the degree and quality of light used on the stage. Appia used to demonstrate this by the scene from the opera of *Romeo and Juliet* in which the two lovers meet at Capulet's ball. Just by taking down all the lights on the stage and focusing on the two lovers, the designer can help to emphasize the intensity of the moment in the same way that the score does. Again, in Wagner's *Tristan und Isolde* which he designed for the Scala, Milan, instead of setting the second act in moonlit darkness (the scene in a garden at night), because he wanted to convey the radiance in the souls of the lovers he had the stage bathed with a warm, almost supernatural light as though night, although it surrounded the lovers, did not exist for them. For Appia light served not merely to illuminate what was happening on stage but to highlight the emotional mood of a scene from moment to moment. This called for an elaborate lighting plot which would stand in relation to a play as music does to an opera. Of course all this is standard practice today but in 1897 it was highly experimental.

One of the first people to experiment with light was Loie Fuller, the American dancer, who at the turn of the century was very much a sensation in Paris. Rodin referred to her as 'a woman of genius'. Of all her dances, perhaps the most popular was the Fire Dance. For this fourteen electricians were necessary, directed by means of gestures, taps of her heel and other signals worked out between them. The effect of flame and smoke was produced by the play of light on the whirling folds of material, especially from below, as she danced on glass. This innovation, a pioneer realization of indirect lighting, was acclaimed as an effect 'greater than Bayreuth', and was the inspiration for the famous lithograph by Toulouse-Lautrec.

Jean Mercier recalls being with Toscanini when the latter was looking at Appia's designs for *Tosca*, which were then being executed for the Scala, Milan. *'Ça chante!'* was Toscanini's smiling comment.

Perhaps because music was his chief inspiration, Appia did not seek to impose his abstract sets upon realistic plays but limited his reforms to opera and to Shakespeare. Unlike Craig, he insisted upon the importance of the actor. It was because he considered painted scenery two-dimensional and the actor three-dimensional that he opposed the traditional form of scenery. His designs, consisting mainly of rostra, columns, flights of steps, etc., provided, with the aid of light, an environmental and three-dimensional use of space in which the actor could feel at ease.

In 1914 Appia and Craig shared the place of honour at the International Theatre Exhibition at Zurich. At that time they did not know each other. Craig went to meet Appia at the station. They recognized each other almost by instinct and, while Appia was still some way off, Craig held out his arms in a gesture of welcome which was magnified by the folds of his cape, like the wings of a bird.

Although Appia could not speak English, and Craig knew no French, they carried on a lively conversation over lunch, covering the tablecloth with drawings and diagrams. At one point Craig wrote his name on the tablecloth and next to it that of Appia, over the top of which he wrote the word 'music', and then drew a circle around it. As Jean Mercier comments, it was a perfect symbol of the difference between the two artists. 'The reform of Appia was dominated and directed by a major force—music. Hence the circle which circumscribed and limited the name of Appia, while that of Craig had a freedom which spread to the limits of the cloth!'

Like Craig, Appia mounted less than a dozen productions in his lifetime. A perfectionist, he was continually frustrated by the structure of most modern theatres. He realized that dramatic art could only be reformed by first reforming the place where that art develops.

'The arbitrary conventions of our auditoriums and stages placed face to face still control us!' he wrote. 'Let us leave our theatres to their dying past and let us construct elementary buildings designed merely to cover the space in which we work.'

People came from all over the world to visit Appia, yet Craig was to steal much of the limelight because he was the better draughtsman as well as a writer with a more infectious style. Craig was an extravert, Appia an introvert. Craig was also an actor and therefore dramatized everything he did or said. In a sense, his meeting with Appia, when he lifted his arms like a great bird and enveloped Appia in his wings, is a very apt image of the two men. Craig is remembered—yet, in most of his ideas, Appia had already anticipated him. But among such artists there is no question of competition. As Stanislavsky says: 'In different corners of the world, due to conditions unknown to us, various people in various spheres sought in art for the same naturally born creative principles. Upon meeting they were amazed at the common character of their ideas.'

8 Copeau—le petit pauvre

At the beginning of the twentieth century Gertrude Stein and
Erik Satie were seeking for a freshness and a childlike simplicity
in their work. Gertrude Stein, who spoke of 'beginning again and
again', explored the relationships of words, parts of speech and
the use of the present tense. Satie went back as far as medieval
and Greek modes of composition, eschewing sonorities and
attempting to make every note audible. Brancusi, the sculptor,
was also seeking for a greater simplicity in his work. He would
take a single form, such as the egg, as the basis of his sculpture.
These three, united by a common search for the primal in art,
became close friends.

In France Jacques Copeau founded the Théâtre du Vieux-
Colombier in 1913. He was intent on freeing the stage from cum-
bersome machinery and showy effects. 'Those who get lost in the
facile byways of decoration and refinements of lighting, with the
pretence of "total art", are on the wrong road,' he wrote.

He was also rebelling against the artificial rhetoric of classical
productions at the Comédie Française, as well as against the
excessive naturalism of Antoine at the Théâtre Libre. Yet his
Essai de Rénovation Dramatique is curiously unlike the usual
manifesto written by someone launching a theatre. Modestly he
sets forth his ideas.

We do not represent a school. We bring with us no formula in the belief
that from it there must inevitably spring the theatre of tomorrow.
Herein lies a distinction between us and those enterprises that have
gone before us. These—and it can be said without offence to the best
known among them, the Théâtre Libre, and without belittling the
achievements of its director, André Antoine, to whom we owe so much
—these fell into the imprudent and unconscious mistake of limiting
their field of action by a programme of revolution. . . We do not know
what is to be the theatre of tomorrow but in founding the Theatre of the
Vieux-Colombier we are preparing a place and haven of work for tomorrow's inspiration.

Almost the symbol of Copeau's point of departure, of going
back to first sources, was his theatre, startlingly simple and open,
without footlights or proscenium arch. Décor was used sparingly,
the atmosphere for each play being created almost entirely by
lighting and the addition of one or two key properties. Granville-
Barker, a close friend and admirer, wrote to him—'The art of the
theatre is the art of acting, first, last, and all the time. You very
soon found that out.'

The acting in a modern play was, Norman Marshall recalls, at
first sight completely realistic, yet business was reduced to a
minimum, each gesture was used selectively and thereby gained
in significance. Copeau achieved a reality beyond the naturalism of
Antoine or that of the early productions of the Moscow Art

Theatre. When in 1920 Copeau staged a realistic play by Charles Vildrac, Antoine, who was then a drama critic, was astonished by the kind of reality he saw depicted on the stage. The action took place in a seamen's café. There was a door at the back through which the sea was suggested by means of light. There was a counter, three tables and ten chairs. That was all. 'The atmosphere,' wrote Antoine, 'is created with an almost unbearable intensity. . . The public is no longer seated in front of a picture, but in the same room alongside the characters. This extraordinary impression has never before been produced to this extent, such a complete elimination of all "theatrical elements" makes for detailed perfection in acting.'

In 1913 Copeau had ended his manifesto with these famous words—'*Pour l'oeuvre nouvelle qu'on nous laisse un tréteau nu!*' And in one of his most famous productions, Molière's *Les Fourberies de Scapin*, the action was set on a bare platform built of wood, isolated in the centre of the stage and violently lit from above by a large triangle of lights hung in full view of the audience. As in the Kabuki Theatre, the platform could represent the inside of a house, a palace, a battle-camp and the area around it, a garden surrounding a house, a lake surrounding an island, or a lower level of the house. Again, as in the Kabuki, such a setting called for movement and speed from the actors; acting of a really physical kind.

Copeau had a great sense of choreography but it was not imposed from without, as the invention of a brilliant showman, but developed organically from the text. 'The one originality of interpretation which is not anathema,' he would tell his students, 'is that which grows organically from a sound knowledge of the text.' He was deeply sensitive to the underlying rhythms of a text, the intervals of time and the elements in drama which were similar to music. Again, there is a parallel with the Kabuki where music, in some form or another, underlies and sustains the rhythm of the play. Even in silent pantomime in Kabuki there is a basic underlying beat. For each of his rôles the late Nakamu Baigyoku would set a basic regularity of pulse and, with almost metronomical precision, maintain it by his acting and movements. Michel Saint-Denis, who succeeded Copeau, his uncle, at the Vieux-Colombier, inherited this sense of musical structure in a play, and would rehearse certain scenes with a stop-watch.

Copeau came late to the theatre. For many years a drama critic, he was thirty-five when he began to direct. André Gide, in his Journal for 10 July 1905, had written, 'Copeau, at twenty-seven, seems ten years older; his over-expressive features are already worn out by suffering. His shoulders high and firm like those of someone who takes much upon himself.'

The existence of the Vieux-Colombier under Copeau was very short: seven months from 1913–14; then, during the war, a period of two years in New York at the Garrick Theatre, presenting the company in over fifty productions; and finally, five years from 1919–24. This brief period was none the less to have a profound influence upon the French theatre—'Copeau was the seed from which we all grew,' commented Jean-Louis Barrault on the occasion of Copeau's death—and upon theatre in Europe and America.

In 1924 Copeau closed the Vieux-Colombier and withdrew to Burgundy with a company of young actors because he felt they must renew their strength by 'kissing the soil'. There they worked on themes without texts, improvised with masks, rehearsed a Japanese Noh play—because, as he said, 'it is the most disciplined form we know,'—and in contrast with this studied the spontaneous skills required by the Commedia dell' Arte. He worked with his young pupils rather like children with whom, away from the influence of the more sophisticated and somewhat resentful members of the company, he hoped to re-discover the secrets of acting. He laid great stress upon the physical and technical expertise of the actor, and wanted his students to feel free to use mime, dance, acrobatics, improvisation, as a means of dramatic expression.

In 1922, before their retreat to the country, Stanislavsky had come with the Moscow Art Theatre to the Théâtre des Champs-Elysées in Paris. All Copeau's students went to see the famous Russian troupe, 'a little ready to laugh in advance', Michel Saint-Denis recalls. 'We were going to see those realists, those naturalistic people, the contemporaries of Antoine! We saw *The Cherry Orchard* that night and we stopped laughing very quickly. . . The visit of Stanislavsky and his company was of incalculable importance to us. For the first time our classical attitude towards the theatre, our efforts to bring a new reality to acting, a reality transposed from life, were confronted by a superior form of modern realism, the realism of Chekhov.'

In 1929 Copeau shocked everyone by suddenly announcing his retirement. He was still young, only fifty-three. Yet his work in the theatre was completed. Michel Saint-Denis was now ready to take 'Les Copiaux' (as they had been nicknamed among the vineyards of Burgundy) and form them into the Compagnie des Quinze. Saint-Denis rebuilt the stage at the Vieux-Colombier, showing an even greater disregard for ordinary theatrical illusion than Copeau.

The Compagnie des Quinze opened at the Vieux-Colombier in 1931. They had worked together for ten years under Copeau. They were mimes, acrobats; some could play musical instruments and sing; all could invent characters and improvise. They brought to the Parisian stage a specialized repertory of plays, most of them created by André Obey in collaboration with the company. The plays dealt with broad popular themes, the plots of which did not depend upon the psychological development of characters. In performance, as one critic wrote, they seemed to bring 'nature' back to the artificial theatre world of Paris at that time. London they took by surprise—and by storm. Audiences were captivated by the clear speaking of the company and even more by their brilliant miming. Norman Marshall describes a scene in *La Bataille de la Marne* in which a whole army in retreat was symbolized by a little group of exhausted soldiers dragging themselves across the stage, so conquered by fatigue that victory or defeat are equally meaningless to them. Of this production James Agate wrote: 'On the stage nothing save a few dun hangings veiling the bare theatre walls, and the floor artificially raked to enable the actors to move on different planes. Off the stage an immense distance away a military band is playing, and in the wings the armies of France go by. We see them through the eyes of five or six peasant women clothed in black and grouped as you may see them in the fields of France on the canvases of Millet.' Agate describes the acting as the kind 'which begins where realism ends . . . the whole cast played with a perfection of understanding and a mastery of ensemble beyond praise. This is great, perhaps the greatest acting, since on a bare stage the actors re-created not the passion of one or two, but the agony of a nation.'

The staging of the Quinze, like its method of acting, dated back to the Molière who toured the towns and villages of France, playing in a tent or *en plein air* on a bare trestle stage. It was this *tréteau nu*, as Copeau called it, which was the basis of the setting used by the Compagnie des Quinze—a light, collapsible rostrum which could divide into four if required to make smaller stages, or piled one upon another to represent, with the aid of a ladder, the prow of Noah's ark. Sometimes one or two pieces of scenery were added, as when, in *La Bataille*, a village was represented by some roofs and a church steeple, modelled in miniature and set upon a small platform in one corner, supported on four poles. The background to the action was formed by a kind of tent suspended from the flies in a ring, which removed the necessity for a cyclorama or wings. In Obey's *Don Juan* the market scene was created by setting up the porches of the houses only and connecting them by gangways with openings in the tent. 'And these porches,' observed Ashley Dukes, 'flimsy and fantastic as they are, contrive to suggest houses much better than the elaborate façades of the scene-painter. . . If they have rather the air of toys, that is fitting because the artists using them have preserved the spirit of children. It would never occur to them that their porches should be taken seriously—as the constructivists for instance take their machines and platforms.'

It was characteristic of the company, and in the tradition of Copeau, that in 1934, in spite of having had a striking success with their *Don Juan*, feeling stale and repetitive, they decided to withdraw to the country. They rented an estate at Beaumanoir in Aix-en-Provence, and planned to spend four months of the year there studying and rehearsing, four months doing open air productions in Provence, and four months touring France and abroad. From July to September they also planned to take ten professional pupils. This ideal life, however, was marred by human frailties, the company disbanded, and Saint-Denis departed to start a new career in England. It is virtually impossible for actors to live and work under the same roof, which is why Grotowski, learning from the failure of past artistic communities, insists that his actors come to work each day and return each evening to their separate abodes and private lives.

The theatre's debt to Copeau can be measured to some extent by looking through the list of the Vieux-Colombier's offspring: in France alone, Louis Jouvet ('I owe him everything,' said Jouvet), Charles Dullin, Gaston Baty, Étienne Decroux, Michel Saint-Denis, Jean Vilar, Marcel Marceau, Jean Dasté, Georges and Ludmilla Pitoëff, Suzanne Bing. It was Copeau who inspired the Theatre Guild of America, as well as the Group Theatre.

The personality of this austere, religious, monastic man who withdrew into a semi-retreat for fifteen years until his death is strangely elusive. He had less ego than any other theatre reformer. All his inspiration went into his work. Yet something of the man is to be caught in this account, by Michel Saint-Denis, of his funeral on 24 October 1949 at the village cemetery of Pernand-Verglesses in Burgundy, where he had lived since 1925 and where, until 1929, he had worked with Les Copiaux.

'I know today that even in the midst of our grief, we—his family, past members of his company, his friends—felt a pride, a serenity which lifted us above our sorrow. This feeling in our hearts, which we hardly dared to admit to ourselves, came to us from the little country church, packed to overflowing, from the direct words of the priest, from the choir of men and women who sang throughout the service, from the four *vignerons* who carried his body from the church to the tomb, from the cemetery hiding among the red and yellow autumn vines, in the place where Copeau himself chose to be. This feeling came to us, too, from the friendly respect of the village people, from the ease in which journalists, famous writers, actors, producers, prefects, mayors, officials all mingled together. It was simple yet dignified, as

Copeau had been in his life time. The serenity there, behind the faces drawn with emotion, came to us through the knowledge that Copeau's integrity, his absolute loyalty to himself and to those things he had set out to do in his youth, would ensure for this man who had left us, a lasting influence which would overcome his death.'

There are some words, written about Charles Dullin (by whom I no longer know) which have always haunted me and which I copied out nearly twenty years ago. They speak to me now of Copeau, and of a man like Peter Schumann in America today.

Une telle foi, je pense, s'appelle l'espérance; non une espérance fermée sur tel ou tel espoir particulier, mais une espérance toujours ouverte, toujours nourrie d'elle-même, qui ne peut donc être déçue et qui propulse vers l'avenir celui qui la détient. L'espérance—un rameau vert entre les dents—la naïveté et la foi ne font qu'une, nous ajouterons que pour avoir une foi sincère, il faut être naïf d'une naïveté qui est aux antipodes d'une attitude précocement désabusée et avertie.

9 The epic theatre—Piscator, Brecht

If naturalism had as its apostle in Russia Constantin Stanislavsky, in France, André Antoine, in England, J. T. Grein, in Germany it was a theatre critic, Otto Brahm, who, inspired by the work of Antoine, became a producer and trained a company of actors in the new naturalistic style. As with Stanislavsky and Antoine, his actors were at first amateurs. Brahm helped to clear the German stage of outmoded productions and to bring it into the main line of European drama.

One of his actors at the Deutsches Theater was Max Reinhardt who, in 1905, staged his famous production of *A Midsummer Night's Dream* at the Little Theatre of Unter den Linden. In 1907 he took over the Deutsches Theater and inaugurated a series of productions which very rapidly caused Berlin to become one of the outstanding theatrical centres of Europe. In 1901 he staged *Oedipus Rex* in the Zircus Schumann in an attempt to recapture that fusion of actor and spectator which had belonged to the classical Greek theatre. From 1915–18 he was director of the Volksbühne Theater, and in 1919 he produced the *Oresteia* of Aeschylus in his newly built Grosses Schauspielhaus ('The Theatre of the Five Thousand') which had an open stage and every possible contemporary mechanical device. It was Reinhardt's hope that this theatre would contain modern life as once the great arena had contained the Greek community.

But, as Helen Krich Chinoy points out, 'Without a traditional way of life, a myth, a ritual attitude or an ideology to sustain it, this theatre was doomed to failure. What successes it did have in its brief existence, and under Reinhardt, were the successes of a director who played on very general emotions through the theatrical devices of light, colour, mass-movement, and music.' Ironically, tragically, Reinhardt's vision was most superbly realized in the massed Nuremberg rallies when the German people were at last fused by a common ideology and a very potent myth.

Like Meyerhold, whom he resembled in many ways—although Reinhardt was by far the more finished, more accomplished director—he borrowed freely from the technique of the circus and from the Chinese and Japanese theatre. It was his avowed intention to free the theatre from the shackles of literature. He offered theatre for theatre's sake and, as one English critic dryly remarked, 'If Reinhardt is not giving us Greek drama, what is he giving us?—The reply is—Reinhardtism—an essence of drama of his own distilling.' As eclectic as Meyerhold or Brook he ran the whole gamut of theatrical invention, directing every sort of play (over 500) in every sort of way. Every production was different, seeking the form within. 'There is no one style or method,' he affirmed, 'All depends on realizing the specific atmosphere of the play, on making the play live.' He could be intensely theatrical, or he could take realism and charge it with poetry, thereby adding to it an extra dimension. In his production of *The Dream*, although he used a realistic set, as the trees, hills and bushes of the forest moved on the revolve, revealing always new vistas, so the forest seemed vast and vibrant with magic.

Reinhardt was both Teutonic and titanic. He was a brilliant organizer of effects, planning a production down to the smallest detail. His teams of advisers, technicians and assistant régisseurs were always at hand. He was the Cecil B. de Mille of the theatre. Everything was carefully noted and illustrated with diagrams in the *Regie-buch*, the prompt copy, which was even more detailed than the shooting script of a film. It was, in fact, the master plan.

At Salzburg, annually, the cathedral, indeed the whole town, was exploited for his production of *Everyman*. For his production of *The Miracle*, theatres in Berlin, London and New York were converted into cathedrals. Again, like Meyerhold, and long before Peter Brook, he was the master of 'total theatre'. Perhaps his most remembered production is, significantly, *The Miracle*, a lavishly-staged version of Karl Vollmoeller's morality play based upon the story of a nun who runs away from her convent: her place is taken by the Virgin Mary who steps down from her niche in the convent chapel. Years later the nun returns, the Madonna goes back to being a statue and no one notices the difference. Meyerhold had already directed a version of this story, entitled *Sister Beatrice*, when at the Vera Komisarjevskaya theatre. The production was first seen in London at Olympia in 1911 and was revived again by C. B. Cochran at the Lyceum Theatre in 1932. On this occasion Lady Diana Cooper played the Madonna, Tilly Losch the Nun, and Léonide Massine (who also did the choreography) the evil Spielmann. Writing at the time of this production, Ashley Dukes, critic and playwright, made the following interesting observations:

Whether the Lyceum Theatre is wisely transformed into the semblance of a cathedral for the performance of this mime is another question. That looks more like good publicity than artistic need. The architecture is effective, a bridge is built between stage and auditorium and, in part at least, the disturbing proscenium arch is eliminated from the scheme of things. The effort to transform the Lyceum implies a knowledge on Reinhardt's part (and doubtless on C. B. Cochran's too) that no existing playhouse is properly suited to large experiments in theatrical presentation. The buildings that are better suited, like the rotunda of a large concert hall or a boxing or circus ring, have manifold drawbacks for lighting and scenic illusion. Among theatres the Lyceum comes as near architectural fitness as possible, and falls far short even when a fortune has been spent on transforming its interior.

He goes on to comment: 'It comes no nearer to a cathedral than

D

to a real drawing room or a real street.' Indeed, Reinhardt, for all his sensationalism, was oddly old-fashioned. Such productions were merely naturalism taken to its ultimate, and stemmed back to the Meiningen Players or the early Moscow Art Theatre productions. For all the attempt to create the illusion of a great cathedral, Ashley Dukes says:

The religious scenes of this mime are, to use last year's good word, 'bogus'. They could never be anything but bogus because the Reinhardt theatre counts among its virtues that of never forgetting it is theatre and never pretending to be reality . . . Why touch reality at the point which is most real to many of the audience, namely real religion? If they are made to believe in it, the enchantment becomes delusion and nothing more.

The proper subjects of the Reinhardt theatre are rich and numerous enough: Boccaccio, Masaccio, Cervantes, Smollett, etc. With such sources the artist-director can do theatrically what Shakespeare did dramatically; he can create as he transfigures.

A disciple of Reinhardt was Erwin Piscator who invented 'Epic Theatre' in the 'twenties and pioneered what has come to be known as 'documentary theatre'. Piscator created a sensation in the 'twenties in Berlin with a series of expressionist productions in which he made ingenious use of elaborate and expensive machinery. He had installed a conveyor-belt on the front of the stage and a cantilever bridge in the centre which could move up and down. Sections of the stage could rise or fall, revolve or slide. Lantern slides and film were projected. Above the proscenium arch blazed Communist slogans. Searchlights played on the audience; motor-bikes roared on to the stage; loud-speakers blared, drums reverberated, machines throbbed, armies tramped, crowds roared and machine guns rattled shrilly.

Bertolt Brecht, who worked first under Reinhardt and then from 1919–30 with Piscator at the Volksbühne in Berlin, described Piscator's as the most radical attempt to endow the theatre with an instructive character. For Piscator the theatre was a parliament, the public a legislative body. He did not want merely to provide his audience with an aesthetic experience but to stimulate them to take a practical stand in matters concerning their own welfare and that of their country. All means to this end were justified. The technical demands of the productions became so complicated and the machinery on the stage so heavy that it was necessary to support the stage floor with iron and cement struts, while so much machinery hung from the roof that on one occasion it collapsed.

Piscator, like Reinhardt, Brecht and many others, left Germany in 1933 and went to America. After the war he returned to do occasional productions. Almost his last, in 1962, was an adaptation of Hauptmann's four poetic dramas on *The House of Atreus*, for which he used a translucent stage lit from below, stylized Japanese settings, screens with back projections, and symbolic orbs of red, black, gold.

Bertolt Brecht, who died in 1956—ten years before his master —was one of the most influential figures in the theatre since the 'thirties. His company, the Berliner Ensemble, founded in 1949, was a post-war phenomenon. 'Once in a generation,' wrote Kenneth Tynan in 1956, 'the world discovers a new way of telling a story. This generation's pathfinder is Brecht, both as playwright and as director of the Berliner Ensemble.'

For Brecht the purpose of drama was 'To teach us how to survive'. Instead of audiences feeling, they were to think. To this end he expected his actors to present a case rather than identify emotionally with the characters they were portraying. In order to 'alienate' the audience, to create an effect of distancing, he would terminate a scene before its climax; at appropriate intervals slides would be projected, bearing a message which served to underline the point of a scene. In various ways he would constantly interrupt the action, and the low white curtains would be drawn across at the end of every scene. By means of this 'alienation' the spectator, so he maintained, would be enabled to ponder the action, draw his own conclusions, and so become a more useful member of society.

It is ironic and also, as Ernest Bornemann pointed out, the ultimate paradox that Brecht's theatre remained to the last a delight for those who were susceptible to his lyricism.

Every device which he used to destroy the 'magic' of theatre became magic in his hands. The exposed stage lights, far from alienating us, communicated all of Brecht's love for the stage. . . The very rhythm of interruptions became a poetic pattern and destroyed the purpose for which they had ostensibly been conceived. . .

The tragedy of Brecht's life boils down to this simple fact: he gained the admiration and respect of those whom he professed to despise—the poets, the intellectuals, the West; and he failed to gain the one audience in the world for whom he claimed to write: the working class, the Party, the East.

In England, Joan Littlewood was to experience a similar success and failure.

When Brecht left Germany in 1933 with his wife and two small children, he was to spend the next eight years in exile, always in unbelievable poverty, journeying through Austria, Denmark, Sweden, Finland, Russia, France, England, Switzerland, finally, in 1941, settling in America. In 1947 he was called before the Committee of Un-American Activities and in that same year he returned to Germany.

In 1940 he was in Finland where he appropriated a Finnish classic play, *Puntila*, and re-shaped it as his own drama, much as he was to do with Shakespeare's *Coriolanus*. In October of that year he lectured to students in Helsinki on the subject of experimental theatre. What he had to say on that occasion shows how profoundly he was aware of his place in the tradition of Western theatre, and of the direction in which he was travelling.

In reviewing the experiments of Antoine, Brahm, Jessner, Stanislavsky, Craig, Reinhardt, Meyerhold, Vakhtangov and Piscator, he showed how they had enlarged the possibilities of expression in the theatre. Against this general background, and within the particular framework of his experience with Piscator, he went on to explain his ideas, which had begun to be developed in Berlin and were to be fully realized in the work of the Berliner Ensemble after the war. The heterogeneous experiments of half a century were seen at last to have found a common base.

'Is this new style of production *the* new style?' he questioned. 'Is it a technique which is complete and which can be surveyed as such, the definitive result of all these experiments? The answer is: no. It is *one* way, the way in which *we* have gone. Experiments must continue. The same problem exists for all art, and it is a gigantic one.'

10 The theatre of ecstasy—Artaud, Okhlopkov, Théâtre Panique

'If people are out of the habit of going to the theatre,' wrote Antonin Artaud, 'it is because we have been accustomed for four hundred years, that is since the Renaissance, to a purely descriptive and narrative theatre—story-telling psychology.'

It was in 1925, the same year that Peter Brook was born, that Artaud began to be involved with the Surrealist movement. In 1927, with Roger Vitrac, he founded the Théâtre Alfred Jarry where for two years they did experimental productions. In 1931, at the Colonial Exhibition in Paris, Artaud saw the Balinese dancers who were to have a profound influence upon his concept of theatre. In 1937 he was certified insane and was not released until 1946. Upon his release, public homage was paid to him at the Théâtre Sarah Bernhardt, and among those present were Charles Dullin, Colette, Roger Blin, Jean-Louis Barrault and Jean Vilar. He died two years later.

Some of Artaud's ideas were, of course, not original; they had already been pioneered by Appia, Meyerhold and Reinhardt. The last two had experimented with breaking down the barrier between audience and actors, while Meyerhold had demonstrated again and again that theatre was a creative act in itself, and not simply the illustration of a dramatic text. The point is, however, that Artaud was discovering these things for himself and for the French theatre. As Ionesco says, 'I think one discovers more than one invents, and that invention is really discovery or re-discovery'.

It is important to stress this. So often the work of a director is hailed as being original; an 'experiment' is described in the press as an important breakthrough to new forms; or a young director talks about the use of a particular technique, perhaps the use of film in the theatre, as though this were being done for the first time. Truly experimental work that has an organic, and not merely a spasmodic growth can only be arrived at in the light of what has already been achieved by other workers in the field. In order to move forward one must first be able to look back. A knowledge of what has been achieved at different times in different parts of the world strengthens a sense of tradition, of one's roots. Truly creative minds, such as Grotowski or Brecht, acknowledge their debt to the past. Such men build on what they find. We cannot escape our debt to the past even when it is necessary to break with it.

A sense of history creates a sense of humour, a sense of humility even: we are less inclined to appropriate to ourselves the credit for certain techniques or discoveries. In the 'fifties Happenings were all the rage, fathered at that period by John Cage who, in 1952, gave one of his first Happenings during which, the audience seated in the middle, various activities took place simultaneously. David Tudor played the piano, John Cage lectured from a rostrum,

Robert Rauschenberg played a victrola, Charles Olson talked, and Merce Cunningham danced. Yet this was by no means the first Happening: way back in 1916–21 the Dadaists were at it! At one such Happening in Zurich, tin cans and keys were jangled as musical accompaniment; someone placed a bouquet of flowers at the feet of a dressmaker's dummy; Arp's poems were declaimed from inside an enormous hat; Huelsenbeck roared out his poems, while Tzara beat time on a packing case. These last two also waddled about inside a sack, yapping like bear cubs, their heads pushed into a pipe.

If in the 'thirties Artaud was announcing that 'the theatre will never find itself again except by furnishing the spectator with the truthful precipitates of dreams', Stanislavsky at the turn of the century was already seeking a theatre that would 'picture not life itself as it takes place in reality, but as we vaguely feel it in our dreams'.

Artaud's vision of a theatre which would be something more than mere spectacle had already been crystallized by Appia— 'How can we once more live art instead of merely contemplating works of art?', and by Craig—'The theatre of the future will be a theatre of visions, not a theatre of sermons nor a theatre of epigrams.'

It is important to remember that Artaud, writing a quarter of a century later, was rebelling against a particular kind of rhetorical acting then fashionable at the Comédie Française. He was attacking a French theatre particularly dominated by words, by reverence for the author. In place of the poetry of language, he was now proposing a poetry of space, employing such means as music, dance, painting, kinetic art, mime, pantomine, gesture, chanting, incantations, architectural shapes, lighting. He writes:

I am well aware that the language of gestures and postures, dance and music, is less capable of analysing a character, revealing a man's thoughts, or elucidating states of consciousness clearly and precisely than is verbal language, but whoever said the theatre was created to analyse a character, to resolve the conflicts of love and duty, to wrestle with all the problems of a topical and psychological nature that monopolize our contemporary stage?

In order to emphasize his break with the contemporary stage Artaud proposed, 'abandoning the architecture of present-day theatres. We shall take some hangar or barn, which we shall have reconstructed according to processes which have culminated in the architecture of certain churches or holy places, and of certain temples in Tibet.' In this he was following in the steps of Appia who had already foreseen that the dramatic art could not be reformed without first reforming the *place* where that art takes place. 'The arbitrary conventions of our auditoriums and stages placed face to face still control us!' Appia had written. 'Let us leave our theatres to their dying past, and let us construct elementary buildings, designed merely to cover the space in which we work.'

It was working on this principle that, in 1920, Jacques Copeau started his School of the Vieux-Colombier in Paris with the most rudimentary equipment. In 1924 he closed his theatre in Paris and left for Burgundy with his young actors. Their workroom there was a large hall used normally for storing surplus barrels of wine. No distinction was made between stage and auditorium. The floor was given a coating of cement on which was drawn a vast network of lines forming geometric patterns necessary for their work, providing a play of directing lines which helped to maintain a perfect harmony in the various groupings. When, in 1929, the company returned to Paris under the leadership of Michel Saint-Denis, the first thing they did was to erect a similar studio at Sèvres. 'Working in such a scenic space,' commented Appia, who followed the work of the company with great interest, 'gives the material a malleable form. It makes it a play of areas of varied dimensions, carefully measured, based upon rectangular forms in opposition to the rounded contours of the body and the curving trajectories of movement.'

Although Copeau had created the simplest form of stage at the Vieux-Colombier, based upon that of the Elizabethan stage, Saint-Denis felt that he had not gone far enough, and he even contemplated taking over a boxing ring in Paris and putting his actors on the central platform with the audience all round—as Jean-Louis Barrault was to do in 1969 with his staging of Rabelais' *Gargantua and Pantagruel*. Artaud's proposed theatre, with the audience in the centre, was to have platforms in the four corners, and a gallery all the way round, so that the action could be pursued from one point to another.

Artaud's concept of his theatre was first outlined in the 'twenties, although it was not to be published (under the title *Theatre of Cruelty*) until 1938. Yet already in 1932 productions exactly on these lines were being staged in Moscow by Nikolai Pavlovich Okhlopkov. Born in 1900, Okhlopkov directed his first production in 1924 in the main square of his home town, using a central platform for the stage, while the audience formed part of the cast. In 1925 he went to Moscow to study under Meyerhold, and in 1932 was appointed Artistic Director of the Realistic Theatre in Moscow, where his productions rapidly became world famous.

Joseph Losey recalls visiting Russia in 1935. 'That year,' he writes, 'Okhlopkov was breaking down the proscenium and presenting theatre in the round and the rectangle and the hexagonal, as it had never been dreamed of before or approached since. Long hours of forgotten talk with this wonderful actor-director-manager and man—forgotten words but the image and effect, never . . .'

Since Losey wrote that, of course, the work of Grotowski and his Laboratory Theatre in Poland has become well known, and it is fascinating to compare the sketches made for the layout of the auditorium for each production at the Realistic Theatre with similar sketches for Grotowski's productions at the Laboratory Theatre.

'The theatre must do everything to make the spectator believe in what goes on in the play,'—was Okhlopkov's central belief. Discarding the proscenium he moved the action into the auditorium as Meyerhold and Evreinov had done, but much more drastically. Sometimes the action would surround the audience, at other times it would be in the centre, or on projecting stages, even above the audience. According to the requirements of the play, the arrangement of stage and auditorium would vary, as in Grotowski's theatre. Further, by having a multiplicity of stages, he was able to develop the use of *montage* in the theatre. Instead of scene following scene in logical sequence, he was able to cut from scene to scene if he chose, sometimes freezing the action in the middle of one scene while he cut to another, and then back again. He also, as in the cinema, used music which was specially composed (just as all the plays were specially commissioned for his theatre) to create atmosphere and underline the action. So much so that he once laughingly admitted that his theatre might well be called a music-drama theatre. The audience cooperated with the actors, so that at the end of every performance the actors applauded the audience as much as the audience the actors. The extraordinary intimacy that Okhlopkov was able to achieve is perhaps best illustrated by a scene from an adaptation of Gorki's novel, *Mother*. The mother, learning that her son is to be released from prison that day, starts to prepare a meal for him. She is so excited that she can't stop talking about what a great day this is for her and what a good son her Pavlov is. As her hands are full and she can't cope with everything, she passes the loaf to one of the audience to hold, while another helps her spread the cloth and lay the table. The actress plays the scene alone and yet, as André van Gyseghem recalls, 'We feel she has told all her neighbours about it, we share her delight, and envy her happiness—those members of the audience that have been actually included in the scene have in some way stretched the veil of illusion to include us all.'

It is to André van Gyseghem, in his excellent book, *The Theatre in Soviet Russia 1943*, that we owe a vivid picture of one of Okhlopkov's productions, showing how the barriers between audience and actors were broken down and both shared in a common experience. Van Gyseghem, with a friend, is in the crowded foyer at the Realistic Theatre, waiting for the auditorium doors to be opened. Suddenly:

the doors are opened from within and we flood through them into—what? Babel. A theatre more full of sound than was the crowded foyer. Women shrilling across at one another—babies crying—men shouting orders—lovers quarrelling—a group of men singing to a harmonica. The savoury smell of cooking assails our nostrils as we stagger dazedly into this hub-bub, looking for our seats. Seats, did I say? We can't see any seats—anyway, they're looking the wrong way, surely?—pardon, madam, was that your child I stepped on? There are some seats—but a rocky promontory has first to be navigated; we dodge under the muzzle of a gun that is being cleaned by a young man singing lustily as he polishes, only to find our heads entangled, as we come up, with a mass of washing hanging out to dry.

They discover that there is no stage. The whole of one side of the long hall has been built up into a rocky, uneven bank, rising to about five feet, and promontories jut out into the centre of the hall. In between these promontories the audience sits. As actors and audience become disentangled and the lights are lowered, the audience realizes it is in the middle of a group of partisan fighters somewhere in the north of Russia during the civil war. By the very simple device of having the actors already caught up in the action when the audience enters so the strangeness that normally exists between the two is broken down. It is as though the audience already knows these people.

The play itself is concerned with a band of partisans which has somehow got itself separated from the main body and is now in the middle of a long trek across hostile country to find and link up with their comrades. Eventually, after a brush with the enemy, the main body is sighted.

'The excitement mounts as the news spreads, the whole company pour on to the rocky steps, shading their eyes, peering into the distance. Yes!—it is our friends, our comrades—and crying and laughing they rush forward to greet—US! We, the audience, represent their comrades, and the actors flood the theatre, the iron stream breaks over us, our hands are clasped by the gnarled hands of bearded peasants, woman greets woman with a warm embrace and the children dart in among the seats, throwing themselves at us with cries of delight. Actors and audience are still one—and we applaud each other.'

The plays staged by Okhlopkov were, in the main, naturalistic in style and socialist in comment, so that, although realizing independently many of the scenic reforms proposed by Artaud, they did not explore the area of the sub-conscious. The Realistic

Theatre was merely perpetuating naturalism in a different format, although Okhlopkov did essay stylization in certain of his productions, drawing upon Oriental techniques.

Apart from the work of Grotowski, which will be considered in the next chapter, perhaps the group which most closely follows the spirit, as well as the letter, of Artaud's famous manifesto, is the Grand Théâtre Panique, operating in Paris in the 'sixties, under the direction of Jérome Savary. In 1968 they presented in London *The Labyrinth*, a production improvised upon Arrabal's play.

The seating in the auditorium is arranged sectionally, some even on the stage, so that the actors can move more freely among the audience—sometimes even crawling under the chairs or, as at one point when the house lights come up and music plays, inviting the audience to dance with them. The 'labyrinth' consists of crisscrossing rows of blankets hung out on washing-lines across the stage and around the auditorium. In one corner of the stage is a water-closet which plays a prominent part in the action—characters drinking from the lavatory bowl, while its flushings coincide with simulated male and female orgasms. The action seems to involve a mad judge, a demented girl, two prisoners and a cruel boss. The performance is improvised, as it proceeds, under the energetic direction of Jérome Savary who conducts the proceedings sometimes from the roof, on top of a ladder, or even suspended upside down over the audience. The step-ladder wobbles, a rope slips, the audience gasps as, sweat streaming down his face, shouting and exhorting, he dominates both actors and audience like a demented ring-master who is determined to be both acrobat and trapeze artist as well.

There is generated an atmosphere of extraordinary tension and excitement. A girl has a real orgasm; at one performance a youth masturbated. There is a great deal of near nudity and, at one point, a young man tears off his loin-cloth, holds his penis in one hand then, grabbing a rope, swings out over the gasping audience as drums beat and lights flash. Sometimes the near-naked actors spill out on to the rain-wet London streets, startling passers-by. In the swinging, slithering, pulsating excitement a goat defecates on stage and a chicken flutters on to a box, mesmerized by the goat. Throughout the action wanders a small boy, the son of one of the company, his face made up like a clown, one arm in plaster. He takes no part, merely observes the action. The audience forgets time, caught up in an atmosphere of fun and exuberance which is a mixture of fiesta, carnival, cabaret and nightclub, fairground, dance-hall, orgy and revivalist meeting. Is it art? Is it theatre? What is art? What is theatre? In London the production was attended by shop-girls and the kind of people who normally never go to the theatre, as well as by actors, writers, critics. It released, exhilarated and liberated. At times it achieved the immediacy of a Chagall painting.

At one point a procession enters through the auditorium. Voices chant, intone, cry out; drums beat and instruments twang. Bringing up the rear of the procession is a tall negro, in a sheepskin reaching to the ground, carrying a live goat garlanded for sacrifice. Smoke bombs (of a sweet-smelling incense) are hurled into the audience by the omniscient director. By means of a rope on a pulley in the roof, a young man is hauled up, upside down, over the audience, playing a flute. The singing, chanting, the ascending smoke and smell of incense, the youth playing the flute and the small child watching, brilliantly capture the extraordinary purity that is at the heart of all Arrabal's writing, especially his memories of his own childhood.

Chagall, in his paintings, will depict people flying around a room, or show a person with his head turned almost off his neck. And in his autobiography he describes how as a child, sitting at the table, he would smell the fish being prepared in the kitchen and his head would fly off to the kitchen to take in the smells. Of his painting of the bride and bridegroom flying round the room he says that they are in the room yet not in the room: their thoughts are flying around in the room because, for the first time, they have transcended poverty and are in heaven in each other's thoughts.

Chagall, like Picasso, gives us what his inner eye sees. It is a question of seeing with the immediacy of a child, for the first time, before labels have been fixed and experience codified. It is like Joyce Cary's description of the small child who, asked to draw a swan, did a light swirl like a cloud for the body and concentrated upon the detail of the powerful webbed feet under the surface which, since he lived by a river, he had often observed. An older child seeing the picture, commented, 'That's not a swan! I'll draw you one!' and proceeded to do a conventional Christmas card swan.

'I say—that there is a poetry of the senses as there is a poetry of language,' wrote Artaud. 'And this concrete physical language to which I refer is truly theatrical only to the degree that the thoughts it expresses are beyond the reach of the spoken language ... All true feeling is in reality untranslatable. To express it is to betray it ... That is why an image, an allegory, a figure that masks what it would reveal, have more significance for the spirit than the lucidities of speech and its analytics.'

Central to Artaud's idea of theatre, which perhaps may more accurately be termed a *theatre of ecstasy* rather than a theatre of cruelty, was his experience of the dancing and music of Bali.

Although Michel Saint-Denis considers that had Artaud been confronted with the Japanese Noh rather than the Balinese company, he would have experienced a great shock of recognition—of what he himself meant to do. Something of the impact which this made upon him may be grasped by those who have never experienced it by the following extract from John Coast's book, *Dancing out of Bali*.

Madé Lebah gripped his hammer firmly; then he and the Anak Agung exchanged a lightning glance, and drum and metallaphone started on a terrific chord that I shall never forget, and straightway we were drowned in the music, drowned, overwhelmed, carried away, submerged. For such music as this we had never heard in our lives, never heard hinted at by the dozens of gamelans which we had already listened to.

This gamelan had a percussive attack, an electric virtuosity, a sort of appalling precision which, as it echoed and rebounded off that long wall, almost pulsated us out of our seats, bringing tears of sheer astonished emotion to our eyes.

Where was the melody? I had no idea! But an incessant cascade of sound rushed through us and around us and deep down into us. The two drums thwacked and throbbed. The deep gongs boomed, the cymbals chattered and clacked; but it was the metallaphones and a battery of twelve gongs of descending size on a long low stand, played by four men, which swept us away. The metallaphones hammered out patterns of such intricacy, such criss-cross elusiveness, and with such a dazzling, brilliant zeal, as was most assuredly outside my comprehension, and from that long battery of gongs came a baffling, staccato syncopation which nothing out of Africa could hope to rival. This music broke its way into us, possessed us.

'Everything in this theatre (of Bali),' observed Artaud, 'is immersed in a profound intoxication which restores to us the very elements of ecstasy.' It is not surprising that he should have been so affected by the unique synthesis of drama, dance, art, folklore, possession, trance, masquerade and religious ceremonial that is to be found in the elaborate ritual dramas centering about the character of Rangda the Witch and Barong the Dragon.

'The Balinese theatre,' he wrote, 'has revealed to us a physical and non-verbal idea of theatre, in which the theatre is contained within the limits of everything that can happen on a stage independently of the written text, whereas the theatre as we conceive it in the Occident has declared its alliance with the text, and finds itself limited by it. For the Occidental theatre the Word is everything, and there is no possibility of expression without it . . . Our theatre has become a branch of literature . . . tied to the idea of performed text . . .

'In a spectacle like that of Balinese theatre there is something that has nothing to do with entertainment . . . The Balinese productions . . . have in them something of the ceremonial quality of a religious rite, in the sense that they extirpate from the mind of the onlooker all idea of pretence, of cheap imitations of reality . . . The thoughts it aims at, the spiritual state it seeks to create, the mystic solutions it proposes are aroused and attained without delay or circumlocution.'

Martha Graham always tells her students that *how* they work, the state of mind in which they approach a performance, is what determines whether or not they are good performers. 'You must be able to empty yourself completely into the rôle on stage. Yet in every performance you must never reach the utmost peak of the movement. Dancing is a state of becoming. The Balinese dance to restore the cosmic balance of the world.'

Artaud, like Craig, stands like a beacon fire, signalling to the surrounding countryside. The great quality of a visionary whose sense of ideal exceeds his sense of what's practical is that he is continually setting before us the possibility of a new direction in our work. Appia, Craig and Artaud are the seers, while men like Stanislavsky, Copeau, Saint-Denis, Brecht and Grotowski are the guides whose wisdom and practical experience enable them to charter these new territories.

11 Grotowski and the poor theatre

Towards the end of his autobiography, Stanislavsky declares that having tried all styles and forms of experimentation he has come to the conclusion that 'all these things mean nothing and do not create an inner, active, dramatic art. The only king and ruler of the stage is the talented actor. There is no art that does not demand virtuosity. But, alas, I cannot find for him a true scenic background which would not interfere with, but would help his complex spiritual work . . . If there is not born a very great painter who will give the most difficult of all sets a simple but artistic background for the actor, the true actor can only dream of a simple board stage on which he could come out like a singer or a musician and interpret with his unaided inner and outer qualities, his art and technique, the beautiful and artistic life of the human spirit which he portrays.'

With these words, Stanislavsky presaged the work of Grotowski. And already there had been Copeau and the Vieux-Colombier.

There was a time in history when men talked of the Holy Grail, but few had seen it. So with Grotowski's Polish Laboratory Theatre. He has fashioned a theatre of exclusivity, hidden behind dark glasses. Yet he is one of the most important figures in the contemporary theatre. His work in Wroclaw is legendary and, as Frank Marcus has pointed out, has been used as a source of ideas by Peter Brook, and by the avant-garde of New York. Like artists working in other media, he set out to ask himself the fundamental question: What is Theatre?

In his search for the essence of theatre Grotowski found that while it could exist without make-up, costume, décor, a stage, lighting and sound effects, it could not exist without the actor-spectator relationship of the 'live' theatre. He totally rejects the traditional concept of theatre which, he says, depends upon artistic kleptomania. As for 'total theatre', this he describes as 'all nonsense'. He rejects all forms of theatre save his own, which he calls the Poor Theatre.

In his book, *Towards a Poor Theatre*, he puts forward several sweeping claims. In providing a different scenic arrangement for actors and audience with every production (he makes no reference to the earlier experiments in this field by Okhlopkov) he claims for such staging 'an infinite variation of performer–audience relationships'. Similarly he claims that 'the number of resonators in the human body are unlimited'. His writings and interviews are an intriguing mixture of naïveté, apparent contradictions and exaggerated claims, totally lacking in humour yet lit at times by such flashes of lightning as illuminate an entire new landscape. No one, since Stanislavsky, has written of the actor's craft with such authority, insight and vision.

Some of the theories which he pronounces are, in practice, often broken. He says of make-up that it is merely the affixing of a mask to the actor's face, yet his own actors, by assuming grimaces, create masks more rigid than any make-up, whereas to watch an artist like Alec Guinness make up for a part is to witness an inner transformation. Again, although Grotowski claims that literature, sculpture, painting, architecture, lighting and direction are all properties of the Rich Theatre, which he supposedly rejects, every one of his productions carries credits for the director, designer of the costumes, properties and what he calls 'the scenic architecture'. Each production is also based upon an original text.

Grotowski's actors do not use furniture and props naturalistically but with the imaginative spontaneity of a child: thus the floor can become the sea; a table, a boat; the bars of a chair, a prison cell, and so on. Although acknowledging his debt to Vakhtangov, about whose work he can only have read, Grotowski makes no reference to Copeau's 'tréteau nu', nor to the work of the Compagnie des Quinze. But, of course, what Grotowski's actors are trying to do is something very different from what others before him have done. For his actors the floor becomes the sea not simply to advance the external narrative (as in the Oriental theatre), but as part of an interior drama. Grotowski is concerned to expose the spiritual process of the actor. By means of years of training and a rigorous physical technique, he brings the actor to such a point of heightened awareness that, as in a trance, he is wide open in performance. 'It is a question of giving oneself,' he says. 'One must give totally in one's deepest intimacy, with confidence, as when one gives oneself in love.'

For Grotowski the actor is a high priest who creates the dramatic action and, at the same time, guides the audience into it.'Here then is a new element in the theatre; a psychological tension between actor and audience; the former trying to subjugate and to fascinate, to charm away every possible rational defence on the part of the spectator; the latter struggling against the "magic" of gestures and words, clinging to logic, looking for some last protection amidst this upheaval of his social armour.'

For Grotowski the purpose of theatre, indeed of all art, is 'to cross our frontiers, exceed our limitations, fill our emptiness—fulfil ourselves.' To this end the actor must learn to use his rôle as if it were a surgeon's scalpel, to dissect himself. 'The important thing is to use the rôle as a trampolin, an instrument with which to study what is hidden behind our everyday mask—the innermost core of our personality—in order to sacrifice it, expose it.'

The spectator, says Grotowski, understands, consciously or unconsciously, that such an act is an invitation to him to do the same thing: this often arouses opposition or indignation because our daily efforts are intended to hide the truth about ourselves, not only from the world but also from ourselves.

If Brecht is concerned to make the spectator think, Grotowski's aim is to disturb him on a very deep level. As Robert Horan says in *Chronicles of the American Dance*, 'If her audiences are sometimes distraught at the imagery of *Dark Meadow* it is because they are so ill-prepared to face the psychological reality which is the basis of her art. It is rather like lighting an enormous bonfire in the middle of an ice-house in which everyone is comfortably frozen. To their distress, the subject of Graham's dances is not dancing.'

Grotowski is concerned with the spectator who has genuine spiritual needs and who really wishes, through confrontation with the performance, to analyse himself. The very physical proximity of the actors and audience is intended to assist the collective self-analysis to take place. Does this imply a theatre for an élite? The answer is a positive, yes. Grotowski insists that this be made clear from the very beginning: 'We are not concerned with just any audience but a special one.'

Grotowski's way of working is to take a myth (national or religious) or some situation that has been sanctified by tradition and so become taboo. This he will attack, blaspheme, confront, in order to relate it to his own experience of life which, in turn, is itself determined by the collective experience of our time—in Grotowski's case, related to the tragic history of Poland. Such a confrontation perhaps lies behind Edward Bond's play *Early Morning*, Peter Brook's production of *Oedipus*, Charles Marowitz's *Hamlet*, and The Living Theatre's *Frankenstein*. Similarly, Martha Graham has explored themes from Greek mythology and the Bible in order to relate them to our contemporary experience of archetypal situations.

In *Akropolis*, Grotowski took a play by Poland's outstanding poet-dramatist, Wyspianski, first produced in 1904, and related it to the wartime experiences of Poland. The original play is set in Cracow Cathedral on the eve of Easter Sunday. The statues and paintings in the cathedral come to life and re-enact various Biblical and Homeric themes. Grotowski moved the action to Auschwitz in order to test how far the classical idea of human dignity can withstand our latest insight into human degradation.

The production is set on a large rectangular stage standing in the middle of the audience. The platform is piled high with scrap metal. A ragged violinist appears and summons the rest of the cast, who hobble on in sacks and wooden boots. The action takes the form of daydreams in the breaks between work. The seven actors attack the mound of rusting metal, hammering in unison, and fixing twisted pipes to struts over the audience's heads. The

1 Gribov in *Dead Souls*, Moscow Art Theatre, 1964

2

3

2, 3   A maquette by Meyerhold and Fedorov for Ostrovsky's *The Forest*, produced in the Meyerhold Theatre in 1924; and a model for Mayakovsky's *The Bathouse*, presented in 1930 at the same theatre.

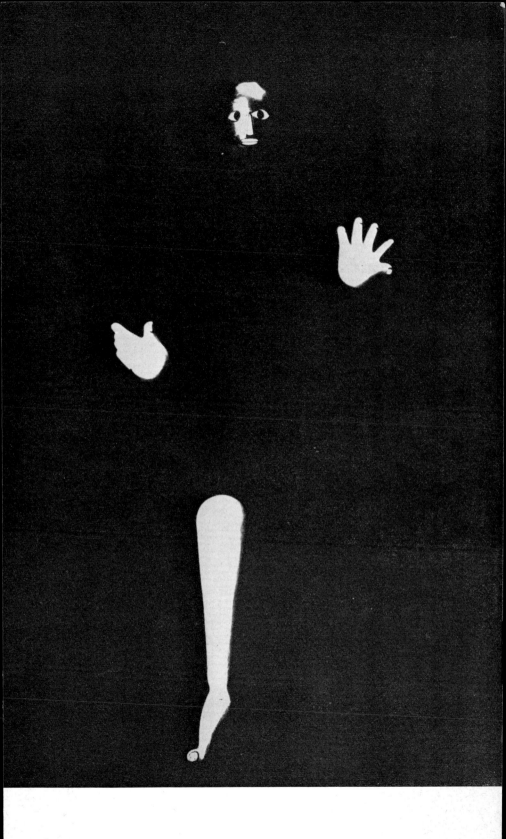

4   Costume for an abstract-mechanical production designed by Oskar
     Schlemmer for The Bauhaus.

5

6

5, 6   Appia's designs for *Little Eyolf*, Acts II and III, 1923

7   Adolphe Appia in 1882

8, 9   Scenes from Reinhardt's *The Miracle*   *Courtesy Lady Diana Cooper*

10   *Mother*, a play adapted from Gorki's novel, produced in the middle
of the auditorium by Zetrerovitch, at the Krasnaya Presnya
Theatre, Moscow, 1933 *Photo: Termerin*

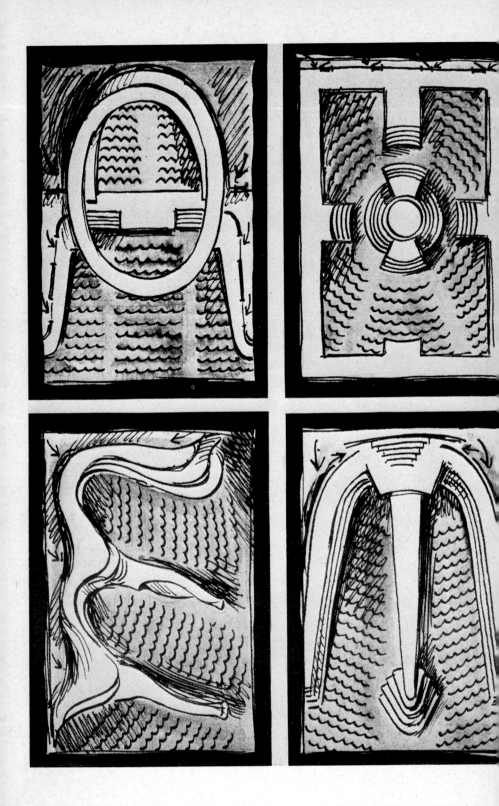

11 Designs by Jacob Schtoffer showing playing areas (white) and
audience areas (grey) for various productions of the Realistic
Theatre under the direction of Okhlopkov.

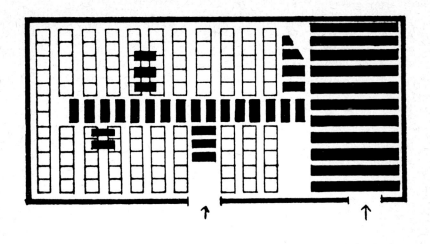

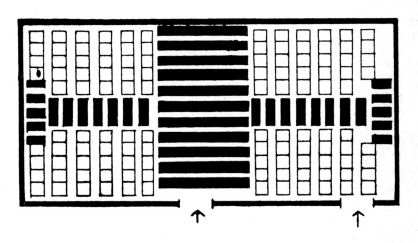

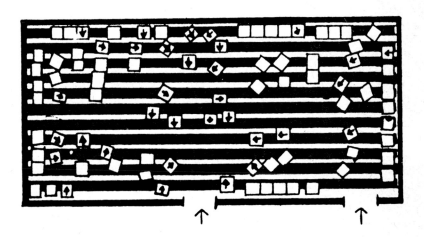

12 Similar experiments thirty years later at Jerzy Grotowski's
Theatre Laboratory at Wroclaw in Poland. The playing areas are
black and the audience areas, white.

13

13, 14, 15 Moments from the Grand Théâtre Panique's production

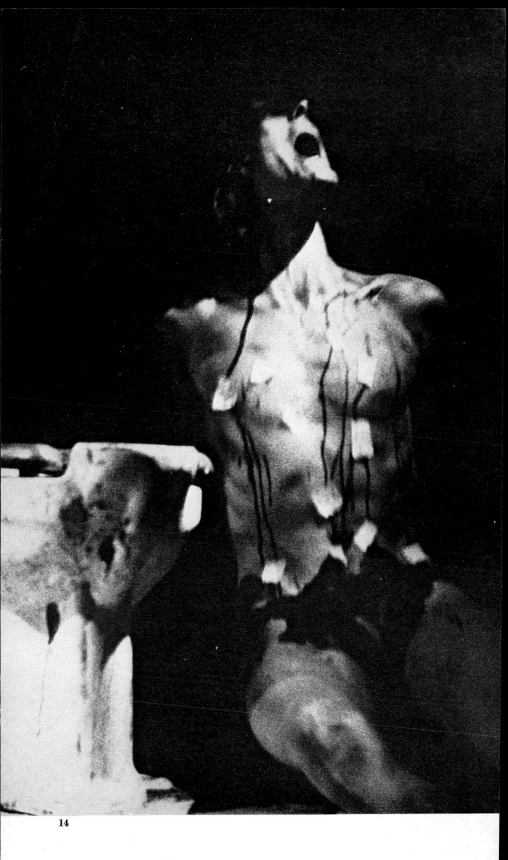

of Arrabal's *Labyrinth*   *Photos: Frazer Wood*

16   Ryszard Cieslak in *The Constant Prince*   *Photo: Teatr-Laboratorium*

17　*The Constant Prince* directed by Jerzy Grotowski based on the text by Calderón-Slowacki. General view of the scenic arrangement. In the centre, the first prisoner played by Stanislaw Scierski. See sketch, fig. 20 *Photo: Bernand*

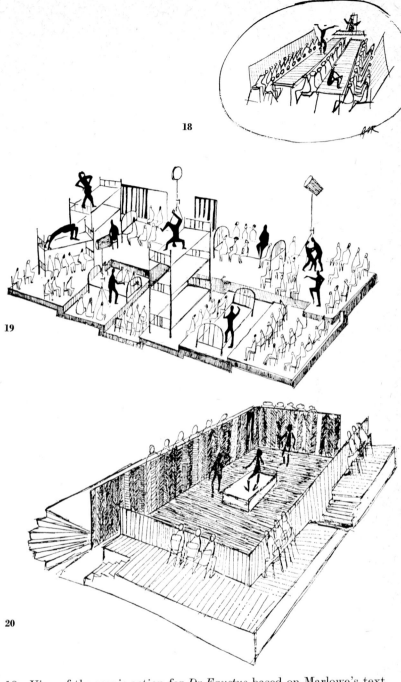

18   View of the scenic action for *Dr Faustus* based on Marlowe's text, directed by Jerzy Grotowski. One hour before his death Faustus offers a last supper to his friends (the spectators). *Scenic architecture by Jerzy Gurawski*

19   View of the scenic action for *Kordian* based on the text by Slowacki. The whole room is built up to suggest the interior of a mental hospital and the spectators are incorporated into the structure as patients. *Scenic architecture by Jerzy Gurawski*

20   Sketch showing the scenic action for *The Constant Prince*. The spectators look down on a forbidden act, their positioning suggesting a bull ring or an operating theatre. *Scenic architecture by Jerzy Gurawski*

21 *The Constant Prince*—Pietà *Photo: Bernand*
22, 23 Rena Mirecka and Ryszard Cieslak in *The Constant Prince*
    Photo: Teatr-Laboratorium

24 Jerzy Grotowski's production of *Akropolis*, Zygmunt Molik and Rena Mirecka

25 Robert Powell, a member of the Martha Graham company
26 Matt Turney in Martha Graham's *Dark Meadow*

25

26

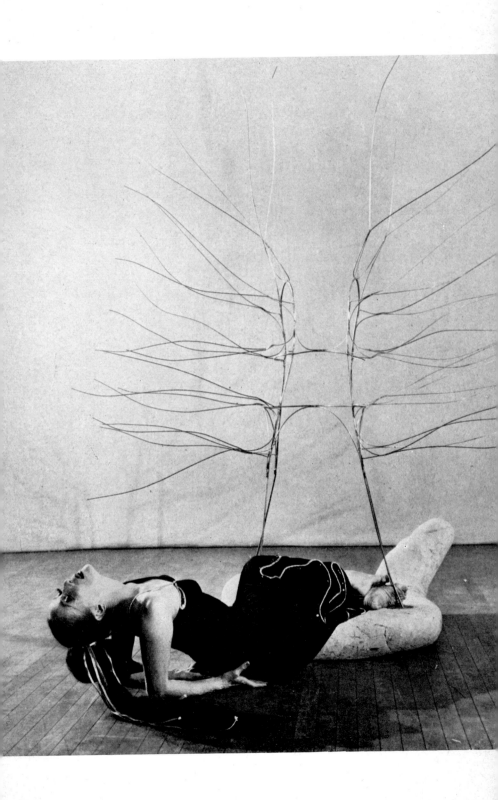

29 Martha Graham in *Clytemnestra* *Photo: Martha Swope*

30 The Martha Graham company in *Seraphic Dialogues* with décor by Isamu Noguchi

31   *Sanctum* by Alwin Nikolais   *Photo: Ken Kay*

32

32   *Sanctum*, a dance theatre-piece by Alwin Nikolais. *Photo: Susan
      Schiff-Faludi*. Note the resemblance to the Barbara Hepworth
      sculpture *Totem* shown opposite (33) *Photo: John Webb*.

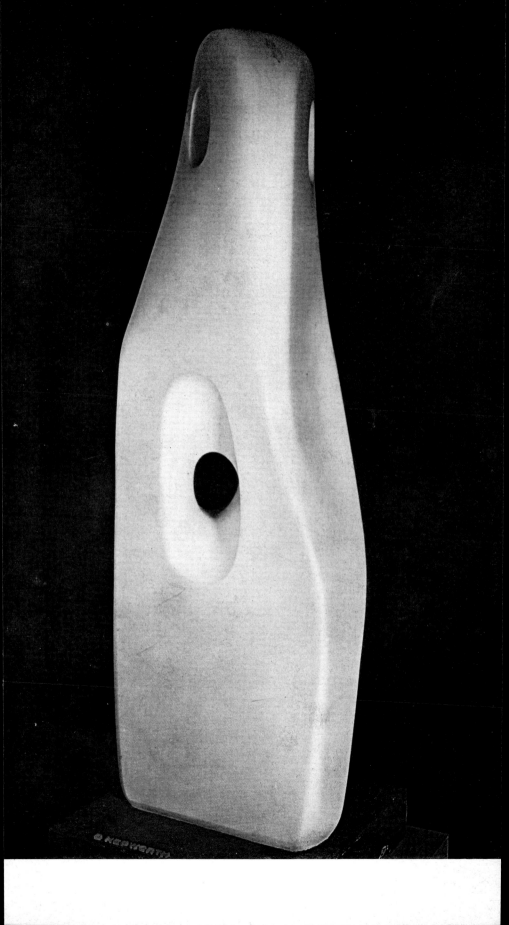

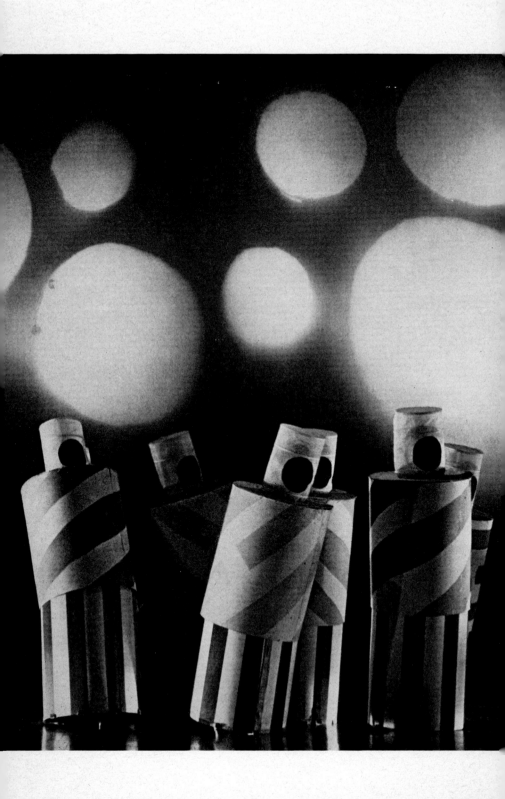

35   *Photo: Susan Schiff-Faludi*

34, 35   *Galaxy* by Alwin Nikolais

37 *Tent* by Alwin Nikolais *Photo: Brynn Manley*

38 *Vaudeville of the Elements* by Alwin Nikolais *Photo: Greene*

39

40

39, 40, 41 *Imago* by Alwin Nikolais *Photos: Robert Sosenko*

44 Bread and Puppet Theatre demonstration at the Pentagon, October 1967 *Photo: Richard Bellak*

45, 46 Bread and Puppet Theatre Peace Parade, April 1969 *Photos: Marc Kaczmarek*

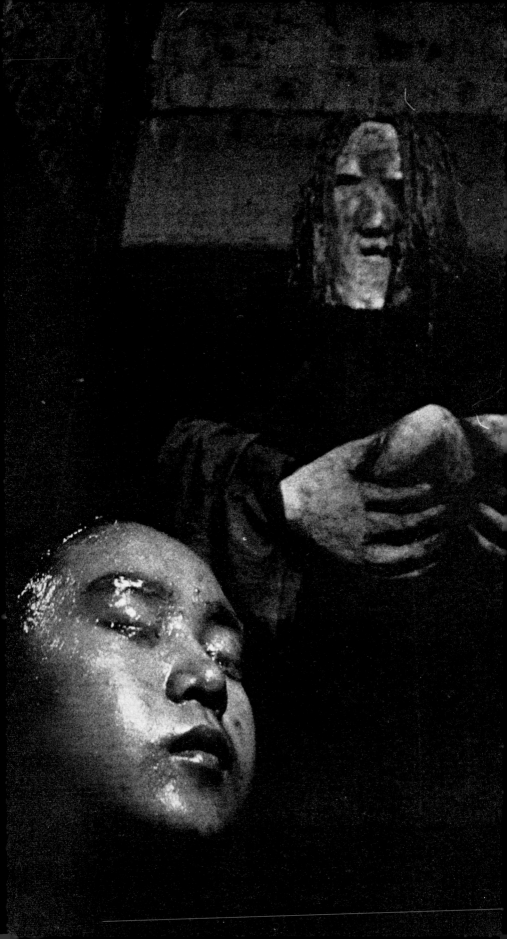

47 Li Min having her face cast for the mask which has virtually
become the trademark of the Bread and Puppet Theatre
Photo: Marc Kaczmarek

48 Margo Lee Sherman in the Bread and Puppet Theatre's production
Crucifixion

49 Bread and Puppet Theatre production of *Fire*
Photo: Marc Kaczmarek

51 Julian Beck *Photo: Jean Marquis*

52, 53 The Living Theatre production *Frankenstein*
Photos: *Jean Marquis*

52

53

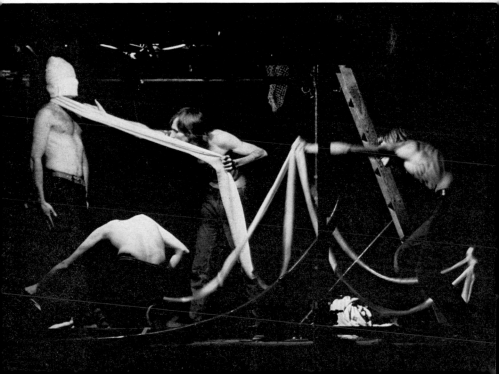

54 The Living Theatre production *Frankenstein* Photo: *Jean Marquis*

55, 56 The Living Theatre's *Mysteries and Small Pieces*
Photos: *Jean Marquis*

55
56

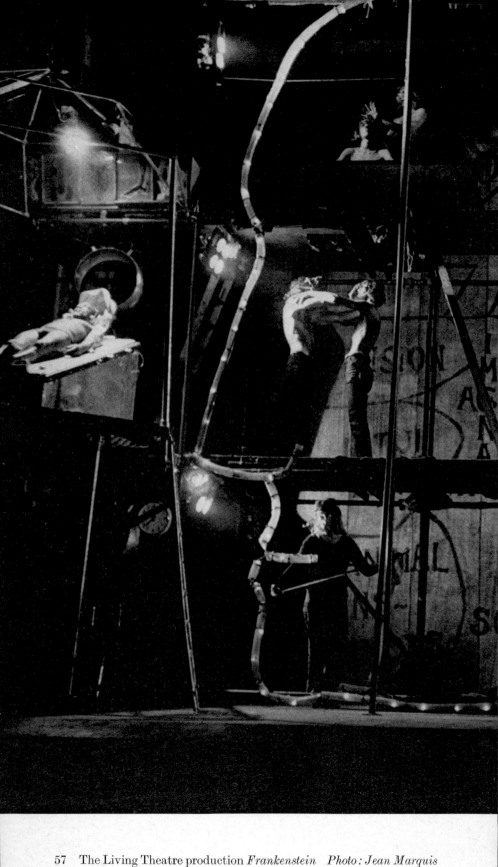

57   The Living Theatre production *Frankenstein*   *Photo: Jean Marquis*

58 The Living Theatre production *Antigone* *Photo: Jean Marquis*

59 'Maze', one of the Myths (audience participation events) at Ann Halprin's Dancers' Workshop. Here the audience destroyed the precise and orderly maze which had been constructed for them, and built their own. They then began to enact their rites.

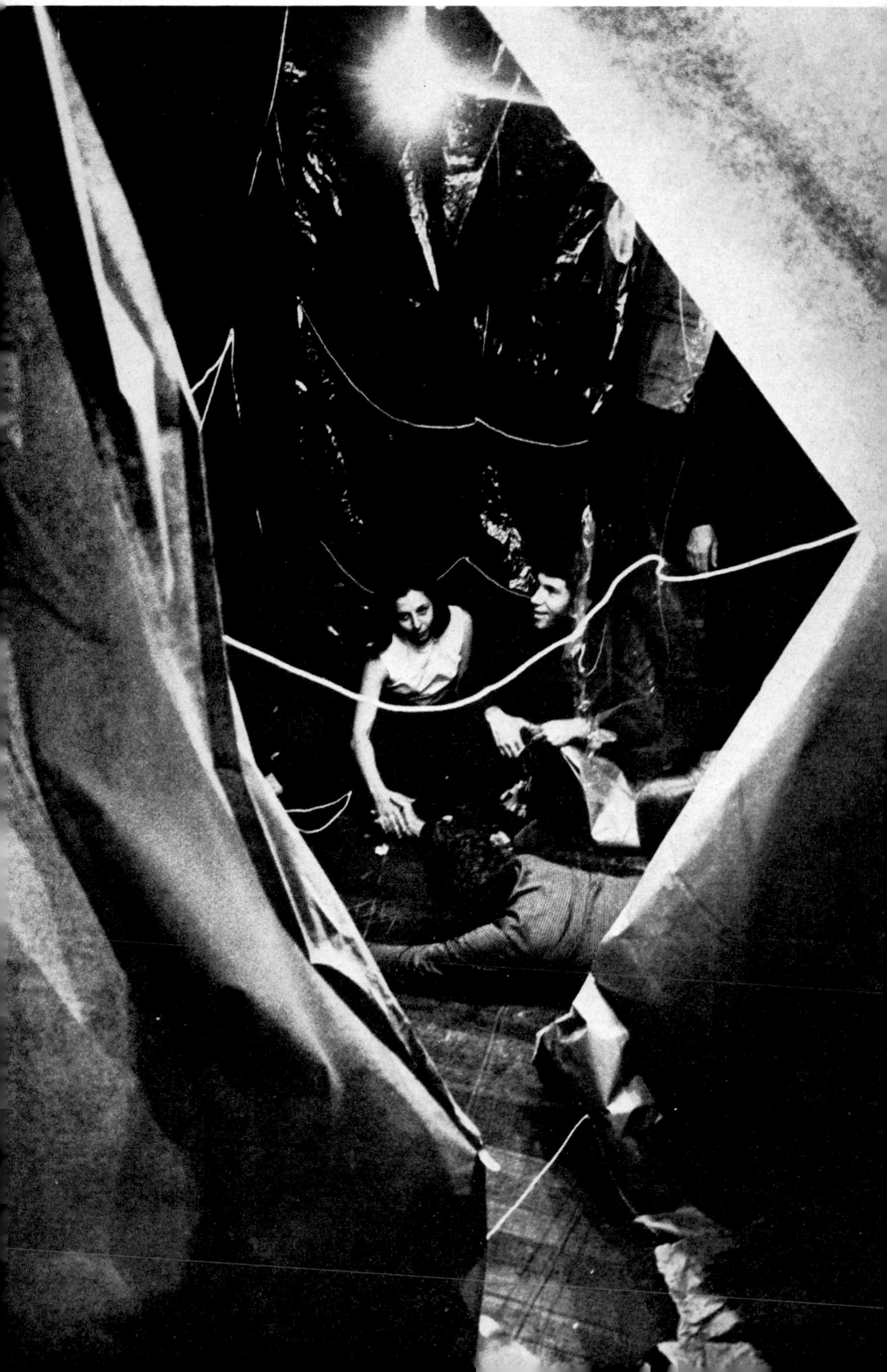

60

60, 61 Covent Garden production of Michael Tippett's *Midsummer
Marriage*, designed by the famous English sculptress Barbara
Hepworth. This was the first time a sculptor was asked to
design for the English theatre.

62, 63   Ronald Pickup as Rosalind and Charles Kay as Celia in Clifford
Williams's all-male production of *As You Like It* at the National
Theatre, London *Photos: Zoë Dominic*

62

64   John Stride as Audrey and Derek Jacobi as Touchstone in the all-
     male production of *As You Like It* at the National Theatre
     Photo: Zoë Dominic

Overpage. 66   The Round House, the home of Arnold Wesker's Centre 42, and the scene of many experiments in English theatre. The Living Theatre performed here in 1969 *Photo: Zoë Dominic*

65   *Saved*, Edward Bond's controversial play about the stoning of a baby *Photo: Zoë Dominic*

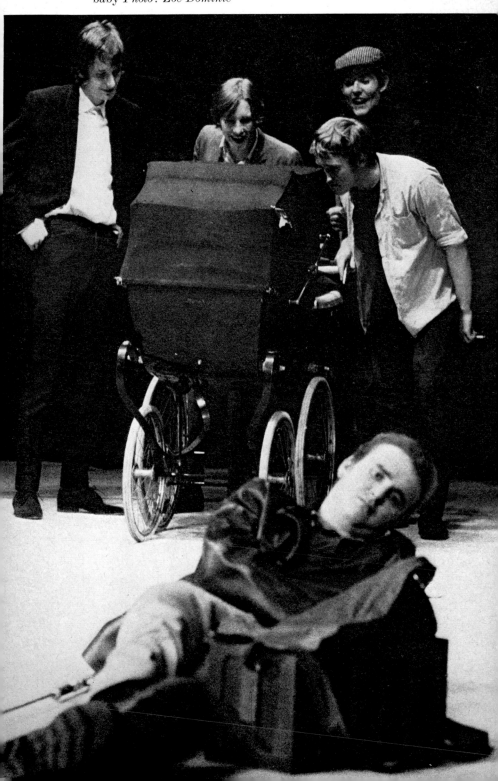

69

69 Scene from Gogol's *The Government Inspector* designed and directed by Jozef Szajna one of the most famous artist/designers in Poland today.

67 (*Opposite*) Glenn Williams, Bill Wallis and Joseph Greig in Alfred Jarry's *Ubu Roi* at the Royal Court Theatre, London. Décor by David Hockney *Photo: Zoë Dominic*

68 (*Opposite*) John Shepherd in the same production of *Ubu Roi Photo: Zoë Dominic*

70   Gogol's *The Government Inspector* directed by Jozef Szajna

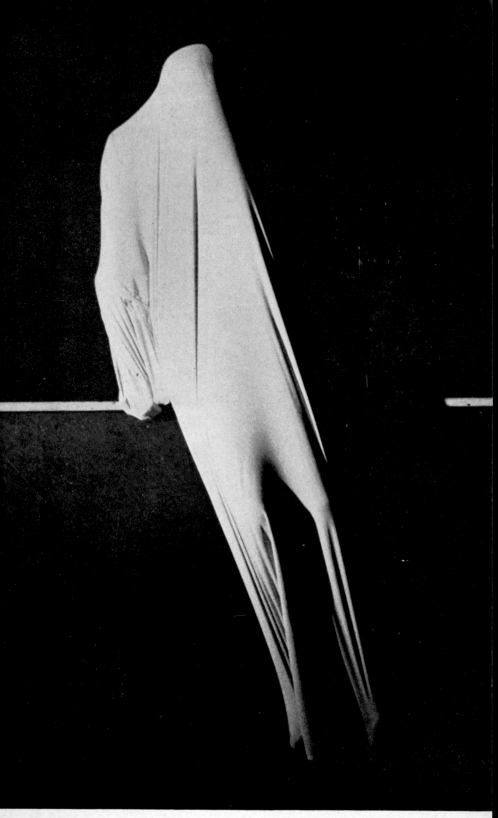

71, 72 Kevin Costello in a sequence from *Death and Entrances*,
the first major work to be created by Stage Two, an experimental

workshop and centre for research started by James Roose-Evans
in 1969 *Photo: Zoë Dominic*

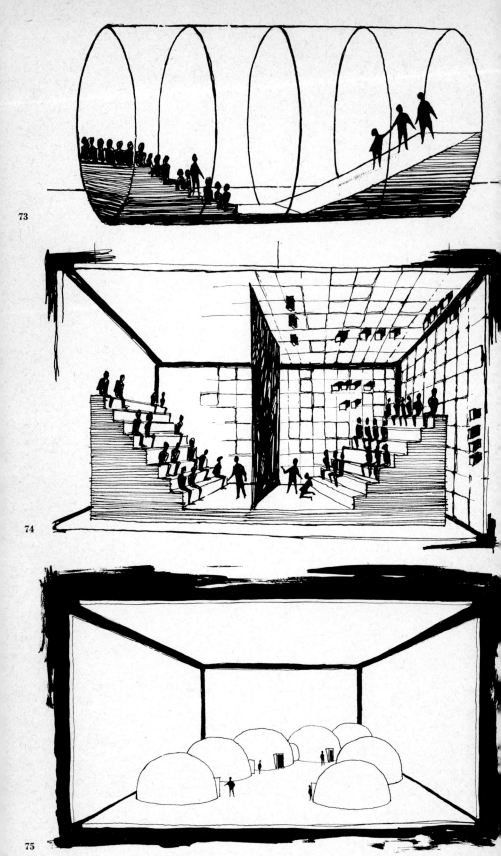

73

74

75

73–75 Stage Two experiments in environmental décor.

audience, however, is not involved. They represent the Dead. In
other productions Grotowski assigns the audience different rôles.
In Byron's *Cain*, they are meant to be the descendants of Cain; in
Kalidasa's *Shakuntala* they are Indian monks and courtesans; in
Mickiewicz's *Forefathers' Eve*, participants in an agrarian ritual; in
Slowacki's *Kordian*, the inmates of a mental home. The question
that arises, however, is how does an audience, individually and
collectively, put itself in the frame of mind and reference of an
Indian courtesan, a peasant farmer, a lunatic?

At the end of *Akropolis* there is an ecstatic procession following
an image of the Saviour (a headless corpse) into a paradise which
is also the extermination chamber.

What is conveyed is an intensely private sense of what it feels like to be
at breaking point. The faces are drawn into rigid masks with eyes that
seem to have forgotten sleep; the bodies, held mechanically at attention, seem to have passed the limits of endurance . . . I can think of few
more potent images in the modern theatre than that of Jacob's wedding
procession with his scrap-heap bride, and the final singing descent into
the ovens. At such moments [concluded Irving Wardle, in a review of
the production at the 1968 Edinburgh Festival] even to a foreign
spectator, Grotowski seems rather to be creating myth than exploiting
it.

Grotowski is at his best when speaking of the actor's training, and
when analysing the essential qualities needed by an actor in his
theatre. 'It is a question of giving oneself. One must give totally,
in one's deepest intimacy, as when one gives oneself in love.' But
such sacrifice is not the uninhibited abandonment which one may
observe in many groups influenced by, but only partly understanding, Grotowski. Grotowski lays great stress upon discipline,
technique, training.

The actor who accomplishes an act of self-penetration is setting out on
a journey which is recorded through various sound and gesture reflexes,
formulating a sort of invitation to the spectator. But these signs must
be articulated . . . undisciplined self-penetration is no liberation . . .
We believe that a personal process which is not supported and expressed
by a formal articulation and disciplined structuring of the rôle is not a
release and will collapse in shapelessness.

One recalls Stanislavsky's realization that for the new art new
actors and new techniques would be necessary, when Grotowski
says, 'The actor . . . must be able to express, through sound and
movement, those impulses which waver on the borderline between
dream and reality. In short: he must be able to construct his own
psychoanalytic language of sounds and gestures in the same way
that a great poet creates his own language of words.'

Grotowski acknowledges, like Brecht, his debt to Dullin, Del-
sarte, Stanislavsky, Meyerhold, Vakhtangov, the Kathakali

I

Dance, the Japanese and Chinese theatre, and many influences. Each has helped him to evolve his own method.

'When we confront the general tradition of the Great Reform of the theatre from Stanislavsky to Dullin, and from Meyerhold to Artaud, we realize that we have not started from scratch, but are operating in a defined and special atmosphere. When our investigation reveals and confirms someone else's flash of intuition, we are filled with humility. We realize that theatre has certain objective laws and that fulfilment is possible only within them or, as Thomas Mann said, through a kind of "higher obedience" to which we give our "dignified attention".'

12 The contribution of the modern dance—Martha Graham and Alwin Nikolais

We have seen how Craig dreamed of a theatre which would appeal to the emotions of an audience through movement alone. In the 'twenties the Theatre of the Bauhaus experimented with plays whose 'plots' consisted of nothing more than the pure movement of forms, colour and light. It was the modern dance, however, especially in the work of such choreographers as Martha Graham and Alwin Nikolais which was to open up new avenues of expression, in collaboration with sculptors, painters and composers. It is significant that Martha Graham always refers to her works not as ballets but as 'plays', while Alwin Nikolais uses the expression 'theatre piece'. Theatre critics, bound by the fixed idea of theatre as word-play, have failed to realize that possibly the most important contribution to the development of the theatre in the twentieth century has been that of the modern dance.

It was Isadora Duncan who first related movement to emotion. Hers was the discovery of the power of movement to evolve its own forms given an emotional impetus. For her dance was 'not a diversion but a religion, an expression of life. Life is the root and art is the flower.' Duncan cleared the way for an exploration of the inner man, what she called 'the soul', so that by the 'thirties dancers were developing individual techniques in order to create psychological dance dramas. The subjects all dealt with the conflicts within the individual; movement was given a motivation from within. During this period at its worst the modern dance became an outpouring of self-indulgent self-expression. Martha Graham, the greatest of the modern dancers, was able to transcend all this, her works depicting modern man in search of a soul, from *Cave of the Heart, Dark Meadow, Letter to the World* to *Errand into the Maze, Ardent Song*, etc. 'I am interested only in the subtle being,' she wrote, 'the subtle body that lies beneath the gross muscles. Every dance is, to some greater or lesser extent, a kind of fever chart, a graph of the heart.' To this end she was to create a technique that would give expression to her inner visions.

It is of the essence of modern dance that the movements flow out of the idea, motion from emotion. The modern dance seeks to convey the most intangible experiences through movement. It is not interested in spectacle as such but in the communication of these experiences, intuitive perceptions and elusive insights. This is not to say that it cannot be devastatingly theatrical, as Martha Graham has demonstrated. Where the ballet is concerned primarily with line and pattern—the external aesthetic—the modern dance is concerned with the basic primal experience itself.

There is a moment in Martha Graham's work *Appalachian Spring* when the young wife rolls about on the threshold of her new home. Referring to this, Cyril Beaumont, who, in 1954 when I first saw the work in London, was the elder statesman among ballet critics, said to me, 'But why does she roll about on the floor at that point? It breaks the line.' In this remark we have the essential difference between ballet and modern dance. Movement is a fundamental element of our behaviour. When we jump for joy or rock with grief, our movements spring from an emotional state and, though they may seem irrational, they contain the essential nature of the original experience, even though they may not be in any way representational. The modern dance tries to convey, through the medium of movement, what lies too deep for words; it explores new ranges of possible, and even apparently impossible, movements in response to whatever demands may be put upon the body by the creative imagination. So, in the example from *Appalachian Spring*, Mr Beaumont was looking for an external aesthetic instead of responding to the inner rhythm of the movement, expressive in this instance of the young bride's joyous and intimate identification with the virgin prairie and the crossing of the threshold of her new home and life. Strangely enough, it is something that Nijinsky would have understood. 'Any imaginable movement is good in dancing,' he wrote, 'if it suits the idea which is its subject.' He demonstrated that what might be thought at first to be ugly or primitive could in fact have its own beauty.

Whereas ballet sought to conceal effort, Martha Graham considered that effort was important, reflective of life, especially life in this century. Thus she evolved techniques of leverage, balance and dynamics that form the greatest single contribution to the idiom of the modern dance. Another of her departures lay in the use of percussive movement, 'of sharp accent and rebound, as of the down-beat of bare feet at the moment of shifting weight; of the off-beat, as of accented leaning of the body in different directions; of short, broken movements that look unfinished yet complete themselves in space'.

In her work she has proved as varied and unpredictable as Picasso. Each season, as John Martin observed, her entire style changed as she discovered new subject matter: dances of revolt and protest; religious ritual and American folk-lore; satire; works exploring the rôle of woman as artist, as woman; and perhaps her richest field of discovery—a Jungian approach to Greek mythology. It is no wonder that, as Margaret Lloyd observes, 'in the public mind today Martha Graham is the archetype of the modern dance.'

Virginia Woolf, in her novel *The Voyage Out*, makes one of her characters ask another, a young writer, what kind of books he wants to write. He replies, 'Books about silence . . . the things which people do not say.' Similarly, Martha Graham has said, 'There is a necessity for movement when words are not adequate.

The basis of all dancing is something deep within you.' And if people are sometimes distraught at the imagery in many of Graham's works, it is because they are so ill-prepared to face the psychological reality which is the basis of her art. 'It is rather like lighting an enormous bonfire in the middle of an ice-house in which everyone is comfortably frozen. To their distress, the subject of Graham's dances is not dancing.'

Above all in the work of Martha Graham the theatre has re-discovered its religious origins. When, in *Errand into the Maze*, Graham as Ariadne comes face to face with the feared Minotaur, she is doing battle with the darkness that is also our darkness (as in *The Tempest* Prospero says of Caliban, 'This thing of darkness I acknowledge as my own.'); she comes to terms with it on our behalf and emerges triumphantly from the maze that is also our maze. In so doing, she is enacting the sacred mysteries of our own times, the ritualistic purgation of our darkness and the revelation of our innermost selves. It is theatre on the deepest level.

With each new work a point of departure for her own questing spirit, Graham has always been The One Who Seeks (to quote the name of her protagonist in *Dark Meadow*); delving below surfaces for the 'why' underneath; agreeing with Picasso that a portrait should be not a physical or a spiritual likeness but rather a psychological likeness. Hers have been what she herself has described as 'a graph of the heart, a blue-print of the soul'. It was not surprising, therefore, that London in the spring of 1954 was disturbed. There were many who hated her work or who ridiculed it, perhaps because it cut so keenly to the bone. As Craig Barton once wrote to me, 'Martha's dancing is about something. It does not entertain or provide distraction. One sees a visual masterpiece in which the dancers move in a masterly and special way, but the reaction of the spectator moves on to another plane of inner revelation, of excited unrest. Even a lyrical abstraction like *Diversion of Angels* has a radiation that shakes one's interior. One has had a serious experience.'

With the exception of a few works such as *Diversion of Angels*, *Secular Games* and some of her earliest solos, Graham has always worked in terms of a story line so that, unlike the work of more recent choreographers such as Alwin Nikolais or Merce Cunningham, it is possible to convey in words something of her art. For those who have never seen her it is worth describing a section of her work, *Ardent Song*. Anthony Tudor told me that for him in this work Martha Graham had transcended all her other dance works; while John Martin, the most distinguished dance critic in America, commented, 'It may well be the richest and the most consistently beautiful of all her rituals.'

With a score by Alan Hovhaness *Ardent Song* had its world

première in London in 1954 and took as its inspiration certain lines from the poem *Winds* by St John Perse—

'—and we have so little time to be born to this instant . . .
The cry! The piercing cry of the god is upon us!
. . .
O you, whom the storm refreshes . . .
Freshness and the promise of freshness.'

The central figure is the goddess Aphrodite, and the work is divided into four sections, each depicting a different phase of the moon, from moonrise to dawn.

At the beginning of the second section the stage darkens. It is now moon-high. Shafts of light fall between the black wings, like moonlight through the pillars of an eastern temple. Three women enter, bound by a single black scarf which covers their heads and is laced under their arms. They move like a constellation in the night sky. One sits and the other two drag her slowly, heavily. They sit, and she drags them. The mood is one of grief and lamentation, the weight of darkness. The women then loosen the scarf and, while one stands on the material centre stage the other two, each taking an end, unroll it across the stage so that it forms a path of blackness across the sky. The light from the wings shines more intensely now, falling along this path, while the women lie full length looking towards the light, waiting, expectant.

Slowly a shape appears, bright, glittering and scarlet. With arms held out in front it advances with majesty across the night. The dancer's hair hangs long and loose and on one side of her head is a twisted horn-like hat. About her neck and in each hand is a two-headed snake—a head at each end of its body. With a drunken lurch the dancer flings it to the ground and stares at it in fascination. As she contracts from the stomach, so her hair swings wildly (Graham has always exploited her dancers' natural equipment as a choreographic extension), her mouth sags; hand, arm and body outline the serpent's curve. Facing front and rising on one leg, the other leg extending sideways, the arms reaching upwards, she falls and lurches about with sharp, staccato contractions.

Thus contracting and releasing, rising and falling, Aphrodite lurches about the stage. It is a lurid, sickening, erotic, drunken and unclean movement. As she gathers up the serpent, holding a head in each hand, so the music quickens and the serpent heads begin to convulse. The body of Aphrodite seems shaken by their violence, the climax of the ejection of the serpent's poison coincides with her own orgasm. The stage is filled with light—it is moon-high—exposing this obscene ritual. Aphrodite crawls limply to a corner where she crouches with bowed shoulders, gazing numbly at the twin-headed serpent, the instrument of her own ecstasy. The sense of thralldom to lust, of the dark night of depravity, the terrible relentless and inexorable impetus of passion, have rarely been so sickeningly and superbly portrayed in the theatre. Only Jean Genet and David Rudkin as writers have been able to articulate this, the dark poetry of perversion.

At the end of this section the lights dim and the goddess re-appears, once again traversing her dark passage across the sky, the serpent once more held in front of her. As she goes, so the three women follow her, the last one rolling over and over on the black material—gathering up the darkness—becoming cocooned, shawled in the dark memory of ancient grief and lust.

At the back of the stage we can dimly see figures, their heads upraised, looking off-stage expectantly. Fingers of light hover over them, touch them and are gone. Suddenly, in a pool of light down-stage, there is a flash of green like that of young grass after a storm. It vanishes; the people wait. Again it appears, farther down-stage, and it is seen to be the figure of a young girl in a green dress, dancing teasingly in and out of pools of light. For a moment the stage is empty and then a youth appears, spinning from be-tween his loins a length of blue cloth which descends, like a shaft of light, from the flies. He kneels and leans back against the material as though resting on the sky. From down-stage right light shines diagonally and in this shaft the young girl appears, carried by another youth. Gently she is lowered to the ground. It is as though she had slid down the shaft of light.

From up-stage, two more youths appear, spinning out great lengths of blue and mauve material, and these three strands are woven into the dance with the figure in green forming the focal point. At one moment the veils span the stage like a rainbow, with the girl seated in the centre as on a swing—the shafts of light seeming to pass through her—while at the back of the stage a fourth youth spins out more and more blue veiling. It is as though after the night of orgy and profane love we have emerged into the dawn of a new love, the essence of which is worship. As the girl travels down-stage towards the audience, the veils streaming out behind her, the men and women, now as couples, all face front with upraised faces and outstretched arms; they are reaching up to the full glory of the new day as the curtain slowly falls. One has the sense of having participated in a ritual of purification, the emergence of the psyche from the darkness of the moon magic into the purity of the dawn.

'In my work,' Martha Graham once told me, 'I have always sought to reveal an image of man in his struggle for wholeness, for what you might call God's idea of him, rather than for his own idea of himself.'

Totally different from Martha Graham in his interpretation of the fundamental concept of modern dance, Alwin Nikolais, along with choreographers like Merce Cunningham and Paul Taylor, sees the dance as moving on to a more abstract or mathematical plane. Already in the 'forties he had begun to have reservations about the psychological approach, feeling that the dance had about exhausted itself on the relation of man to man, needing to find the relation of man to the other elements.

'This is how I want man,' he would say at this period, 'with his arms out in time and space, not folded in on his own aching gut. A dancer doesn't have to emotionalize—he needs to motionalize. He doesn't even have to be a person—he can be a thing, a place or a time.'

At the Henry Street Playhouse in New York, in order to get his students away from 'self-expression', he began to assign them various props, masks and sculptural objects, disguising them so as not to look like people, costuming them like shapes, moving them about the stage like pieces of mobile sculpture.

His dances do not express emotional attitudes or take sides. 'Don't interpret as mad, sad or glad,' he said during a class in London for actors, 'just move. The drama exists in action. Don't mug it. Remember, here the medium is the message!' Although he does not make dances about specific issues or problems, he feels none the less that audiences will find much in his work relating to contemporary life, provided they are prepared to give their imaginations free rein. 'We're drastically concerned about our existence in space,' he says. 'For fifty years we explored psychological relationships. Now we're concerned with environmental relationships and this leads to an even more primal sense. We don't trust any one sense any more. We want to understand by having all our senses coordinated to find a truth. This is why we have multi-media theatre. Your specific references will come out of your own Rorschach. Though I'm probably as neurotic as the next one, I have a free access to associations. Inner visions come easily. Many people have the capacity for this and have long since failed to use it.'

What does an audience see and experience in the Alwin Nikolais Dance Theatre? Certainly it is taken by surprise, caught unawares. Because it is so original you can't really compare it with anything else, any more than you could compare Graham with anyone before her. It is like walking in a new landscape. Each moment brings fresh discoveries, sequences of astonishing beauty and, above all, a rare and exhilarating sense of fun and pleasure. Nikolais is primarily excited by the movement of things, encasing his actors in long shifts, ballooning silk bags, or providing extensions to their limbs in the form of kites on wires, yards of tape, tubular projections, resounding discs on hands and feet, cone-shaped tents. In *Galaxy* collapsible towers enter the stage, the hidden bodies motivating the costumes so that they rotate, expand and shrink. Luminous shapes and masks move across the stage, propelled by unseen dancers. Nikolais' use of light is constantly changing the images, like the effect of natural light at different times of the day and night upon a piece of sculpture out of doors. In *Tent* he employs a white silk parachute which, suspended on slender wires, becomes an enchanted canopy, swirling shapes, pinnacles and clouds, incandescent with colour as it is lit from within, behind, in front.

In *Sanctum* there is one sequence in which the dancers move within a casing of material that binds them at head and feet so that they resemble certain Barbara Hepworth statues suddenly extended into movement, or else 'stand up, still and white, like mummies lined up in a forgotten tomb'.

As with any abstract work of art, the theatre-pieces of Alwin Nikolais can be received on various levels. But most of all, as with all art, they must be *experienced*. We are too prone to analyse and codify our art into tidy cocktail capsules or classroom dicta. Ultimately, it is as impossible to describe the work of Nikolais as it is a leap by Nijinsky or a contraction and lunge by Graham. Photographs give some indication and Nikolais, like Graham, has a stunning sense of theatre. And, uniquely, he has created his own staging, choreography, lighting—every one of the colour slides used in the hundreds of projections is hand-painted by him— costumes, décor and music.

During his first triumphant season in London he sat every night, a solitary figure, on the conductor's podium, in the empty and silent orchestra pit with its black chairs and grey metallic music-stands—his own electronic music emerging from the speakers on either side of the stage—watching and controlling the kaleidoscopic shift of patterns which his teeming imagination had conjured forth. At the curtain-calls he took his company by the hands and led them, laughing and radiant, down to the footlights and back again; his shadow, thrown on the backcloth, shrank and grew with that of the company. One recalled that the company had developed apace with its director, and its leading dancers, Murray Louis and Phyllis Lambert, have been with him from the start. As far back as 1956 John Martin had written 'Here is a group of lively, absorbed and devoted young artists, who have started at the beginning and are learning their way up . . . Nobody is concerned with making a splash; nobody is ready to make a splash and everybody knows it. The only concern is with developing dancers and dances.'

13 Peter Schumann and
The Bread and Puppet Theatre

Frequently Joan Littlewood quotes Noverre's instructions to go to the workshops, the farmlands, the streets. 'The world is full of theatre,' she says, 'It's not in the theatre.' Peter Schumann has interpreted these words quite literally. His Bread and Puppet Theatre, founded eight years ago, seems to me possibly one of the most important groups now working on the American scene. He has quite simply brought theatre to people by coming out into and through the streets of New York with his processions of gigantic puppets and his short playlets on contemporary themes. He feels that too many of the avant-garde groups are more concerned with insulting the audience than with communicating. 'You can't simply shock an audience,' he says. 'That will only disgust them. We don't necessarily have to revolutionize the theatre. It may be that the best theatre—if it comes—will develop from the most traditional forms. A theatre is good when it makes sense to people.'

He regards the audience that doesn't go to the theatre as the best one. That is why he has gone out into the streets. His company is a completely flexible group and its size varies according to need, from fifteen to a hundred for *Bach Cantata*. No one gets paid. They charge one dollar for a performance indoors but nothing in the streets. They do a show for a particular space—the space they happen to be in. The one space they reject is that of the traditional theatre. 'It's too comfortable, too well known. Its traditions upset us. People are numbed by sitting in the same chairs in the same way. It conditions their reactions. But when you use the space you happen to be in, you use it all—the stairs, the windows, the streets, the doors. We'd do a play anywhere—provided we can fit the puppets in.'

They give away bread during or after a show because they regard this as something basic. 'We would like to be able to feed people,' he says simply.

Food, in fact, plays an important part in many of his plays. In one he portrays a group of people at a festive meal and by placing a Red Indian in the centre as chief guest he evokes the Last Supper.

The play (which I saw performed at the Royal Court theatre in London, when the company gave their very first performance in a theatre) begins with the appearance of the near-naked Indian who slowly crawls forward on a plank into the centre of the auditorium and there sits erect, watching the stage. The lights come up on brightly-coloured, childlike cloths of trees and flowers. 'Let the pilgrims appear!' declares a narrator, who then proceeds to read an account of the arrival of the Pilgrim Fathers on 21 November 1620. The pilgrims enter through the auditorium and stand below the stage, laughing and sending up the official record, telling the audience how it really was. 'We didn't find any people

—only savages!' One of them produces an arrow shot at them by an Indian—'We saved it to show you!'

'Let the wind blow on the 21st November 1620!' says the narrator, and the actors blow through their hands.

'Let the birds sing on the 21st of November 1620!' declaims the narrator, and the actors warble and flute and trill.

'Let the leaves fall!'—and from the roof of the theatre descend large green leaves plucked from the plane trees in the square outside.

'Let the first snow-flakes fall!' and pieces of torn white paper flutter down on the audience. 'Now let's start the hail storm!' wise-cracks one of the actors.

A table is brought on, plates, mugs, food are distributed and the Red Indian is invited to take the place of honour in the centre where he sits nobly and impassively throughout the following action, totally ignored by the actors. The company begin to say grace and this develops into a syncopated improvisation with the recurring phrase—'For His mercy endureth for ever.' At its climax the clapping and chanting stop abruptly and cease. Schumann's voice is heard saying—'Who does not give food to all people.' There is silence. The actors remove their outer clothing, smear red round their lips, and then proceed to eat and drink with a concentrated gluttony. For a long time we hear nothing but the absorbed munch and crackle of food, the dribble of liquid poured into mugs. Then the Vietnamese peasant woman in black, bearing her dead baby, appears. She is a recurring symbol in all Schumann's work and the central character in the playlet, *A Man Says Goodbye to his Mother*.

Now the figure moves slowly from actor to actor in silent rebuke, brushing the food from their hands, turning the plates over and placing the mugs upside down. Gradually all stop eating and stand in silence, stunned, lurid blood-red liquid glistening around their mouths. The woman disappears. Suddenly the Indian sings—'When Jesus wept a falling tear.' The play is over. There is silence. The cast slowly pack up. There is no applause. We are stunned. One of the actors calls out—'That's it, folks!' Quietly the audience leaves, though many sit on thoughtfully, or move on to the stage to mingle with and talk to the actors. The entire work has the impact of an early American primitive painting, naïve, intensely felt, a simple yet sophisticated folk tale, sacramental in its impact.

As a play unfolds and you look at the clean-faced, earnest and open expressions of the company, seated in a semi-circle on the stage, all watching intently, thoughtfully, as the action proceeds— you are reminded of a Quaker meeting. Here is none of the aggressiveness of The Living Theatre. You will not find Peter Schumann attacking the audience, as Julian Beck does, as 'mother-fucking bourgeois intellectuals'. And where The Living Theatre attacks the audience because the price of their ticket could have bought a meal for a child in Biafra, The Bread and Puppet Theatre never charge and during their season at the Royal Court Theatre, on their second trip to London in 1969, they freely gave away tickets as well as inviting those upstairs to come and fill up the empty seats in the stalls. If the house was full, no one was turned away but room was found for them on the stage itself.

The atmosphere of a Bread and Puppet performance is set even before the play begins. In grubby white pants and shirts, coloured bandanas round their foreheads or wearing an assortment of headgear, as though they had all been to a jumble sale, the actors process through the streets beating drums, rattling tambourines, blowing trumpets, some wearing giant masks. An actor in a pig's head rolls over and over on the pavement, dances among the traffic, swings from a lamp post, and bows to a dog who is at once terrified! The audience joins in the procession if so inclined, goes for a walk around the block, chatting with the actors. People pause, stare, then their faces light up, smile—the gaiety of the company is infectious. At a certain spot they will stop to perform their short play about Vietnam and then their faces watch intently, rapt, attentive, absorbing its message into themselves yet again. They know that by their stillness and identification they are united with the action, with the sacramental nature of what they are doing. Back at the theatre they file in with the audience. The actors go on stage, chat to those in the audience they know and then, casually, almost inaudibly on occasions, Schumann announces the programme for that evening.

Unobtrusively he dominates the action, hair falling in front of his face, sweat running down into his beard as he roughly grasps a light attached to a length of cable and holds it in different positions, or swiftly ties it to the end of a long pole and elevates this in order to illuminate some part of the action. It is he who conducts the actors when they sing or chant; crouched on the floor of the stage he tells us through a hand mike the simple story of a play as it unfolds. When necessary he takes part in the action, accompanies on the violin, kneels to help his actors climb the step to the stage when swathed in long costumes and in masks so that they cannot look down. Literally he stage-manages the show before our eyes and no attempt is made to conceal by conventional stage-craft the untidy seams or unfinished joins. What he is trying to communicate, his essential vision of man and God, is more important than the superficialities of stage-craft. To see his actors seated on the floor when not in a particular scene, or standing by to make noises and effects, to see their faces, is to know and experience with them the *continuing* nature of what they are about. Their gentleness, their humour, their caring, their concern is part of the total action, more, it is the base and ground from which all their work stems and it does not end with the performance.

Schumann's most considerable work to date is undoubtedly *The Cry of the People for Meat*, his re-telling of the Old and New Testament prefaced by a burlesqued version of the marriage of the God of Heaven with Mother Earth. For this he uses twenty-foot-high giant puppets dancing to the music of a harmonica, with a voice blaring out over a microphone, with all the raucousness of an old-time circus. The birth of Kronos is then depicted as a man-size knight bursts his way through a mass of torn and shredded paper and proceeds to slay his father, tossing the giant head into a red sheet where it is bounced up and down in the air. Two screens are now erected on either side of the stage, one marked 'Heaven' and one 'Earth'. Schumann drags on two figures swathed in sheets of polythene. Holding his lamp in one hand he kneels and blows into the polythene—an image of God giving the kiss of life to Adam and Eve. In the background sit the watching actors and, piled up against the walls, the various masks and puppets used in the repertoire. The stage is littered with shredded paper, torn polythene, lengths of cable, and Schumann scrambling for his hand-mike, his portable light and script. Yet through the untidiness, the mess, the often blurred effects, he carves his blazing vision of man's ultimate destiny, so that the very mess becomes part of the image of Chaos out of which God created order. It is at this moment that Schumann creates one of his most memorable effects. With the announcement of the Flood, Schumann lifts high his portable light to reveal a moving wave of grotesque pigs' heads, the Gadarene swine, mankind at its most bestial. Like drovers at a market or shepherds in shearing time, Schumann, assisted by another actor, moves in among them, roughly binding them with ropes as they pile on top of one another, slithering and sliding forward towards the edge of the stage, an avalanche of monstrous heads with huge nostrils and fangs. Kicking at the heads, manhandling the actors, sweat streaming down his face, he moves in like one possessed against a background of twentieth-century traffic noise on tape, the full-throated roar of modern man. At this moment Schumann carves a theatre image that has all the intensity of Blake. At such moments you cannot but feel he is a 'sent' man, a prophet new inspired. It is as though we were present with the artist at the very instant of creating a work of art.

At the opening of the second half the company proceed to dress up an actor as the Christus, draping a sheet around his head and over his body, placing in one arm the figure of an infant, putting on his face the mask of the Vietnamese woman. As the Sermon on the Mount commences, they proceed to adorn him with various

offerings. 'Blessed are they who hunger and thirst after righteous-
ness'—they bring food and cooking pans; 'Blessed are the pure in
heart' and they hang about his neck a large red heart; 'Blessed
are the merciful'—a garland of fresh flowers and weeds; 'Blessed
are the peacemakers'—a rifle is slung about his neck. The Christus
becomes a focal point for the people's projections and longings—
they hang their sorrows upon him. The actor then mounts a tall
ladder and now, like a tent, there is drawn down over him a giant
figure of the Christus with long hands uplifted in benediction.
From now until the end of the play the actor will sit there, suffering the heat and discomfort. In the conventional theatre the
actor would either shed all those encumbrances or his place be
taken by another actor. Here, however, it is as though by accept-
ing all this that the actor enters into an imaginative identification
with Christ who had to bear the burden of mankind's sorrows.
One is reminded how in the Mass the priest is said to be no longer
himself but becomes the representative of Christ. At the end of
this play, when the actor is revealed his long hair is lank and wet,
his face running with sweat and taut with pain; it is seen to be a
kind of Passion and, as in Grotowski's theatre, a total offering of
the actor in an act of love.

The parables of Jesus are briefly enacted, each given a humorous
political slant. Finally a long table is brought on, covered with a
cloth and laid with round loaves of new-baked, whole-wheat bread.
When the table is set for the scene of the Last Supper, Schumann
and the actors take the loaves and, breaking them, distribute the
bread among the audience, each person taking a portion and passing on the rest to his neighbour. During this, Margo Lee Sherman
stands centre stage reaching up to the enormous figure of the
Christus, slowly caressing the long hands. Schumann crouches
by the steps to the stage, himself chewing, watching with a gentle
half-smile, rapt and attentive, as the whole theatre breaks bread
and eats. The Christus lowers both hands and then the long head
so that, like Veronica with her veil, Mary may reach up to caress
lovingly the sorrowful visage. It is at this moment that a deep
humming note is heard, like a long sustained liturgical chant, continuing for the next ten minutes as tall pillar-shaped figures appear, ten feet tall, swathed in hessian, without arms and sur-
mounted by carved heads of the twelve apostles. As they take
their positions at the table, another Christus figure appears, holding in one hand a papier mâché chalice, in the other a loaf of
bread, which he proceeds to administer to each of the disciples
while the hands of the first Christus, who towers above the action,
descend in benediction upon the scene below. Throughout this the
house lights are full on. Deliberately at this moment Schumann
eschews a conventional theatrical effect, thereby risking laughs—

and getting them—but slowly the unhurried ritual and the un-
ceasing hum compel silence. The faces of the masks of the Apostles
are comic, very human, grotesque even, yet beautiful. They are
our faces yet also archaic visages. The second Christus offers
bread and wine to the first and kneels for the blessing. Suddenly
the table is toppled, there are screams, the great heads are thrown
off and the fish-shaped plane appears in the air, like a black raven,
to topple down the towering figure of the Christus. The action is
both startling and clumsy. Conventionally one would say that the
final effect is bungled, and there are laughs as the actor portraying
Christ struggles out of his costume and appurtenances.

The actors look at us thoughtfully, gently, still rapt in the
mysteries they have enacted. Without manifestos, without dog-
matic utterances, without aggression, this company presents a
truly poor theatre, a holy theatre. Their very materials (apart
from the superbly-made masks) are the creased and old clothes,
lengths of material, curtains, found in any jumble sale. They dress
up in whatever they can find, adapting with the complete conviction of a child. They make do, pretend. One could not call them
professionals in the accepted sense. They bring no conventional
sense of skills, sophistication or polish to their performance. The
plays are presented with a simplicity that radiates from the inner
certainty of Schumann and his followers. One feels that the first
Franciscans must have been like this: it is impossible to separate
the quality of their life from their work.

14 Further experiment today— in America

The traditional concept of art is of an artist seeking to give expression to an inner vision. The artist is concerned, traditionally, to communicate. Of course what is communicated may well be something over and above that which the artist consciously intended. In that the artist's work is the expression of his whole psyche he is often, in Jungian terms, the carrier of archetypal patterns. Further, the reader or spectator may 'read' into a work of art an interpretation that is applicable to his own needs or situation. The varied, contrasting, conflicting and continuing interpretations of the plays of Shakespeare are the most vivid example of this process.

Since the nineteenth century, however, there have been artists who had no message to convey; artists, like Mondrian and Brancusi, for whom the work itself was its own justification.

Atonal music, non-objective art, meaningless Activities, are now the order of the avant-garde while kinetic art, especially when it uses liquids or foam, proclaims an art of the moment—which may even destroy itself in the moment of creation. Definitions as to what is art peter out as barriers are broken down. Just as Martha Graham refers to her ballets as 'plays' and Alwin Nikolais to his as 'theatre-pieces', so we see Barbara Hepworth and Isamu Noguchi creating sculptures which invite movement and a physical involvement—Hepworth recently created a walk-through and Noguchi a walk-on—while environmental sculptors are creating mass and structures in which people can wander. Harry Partch sculpts objects that are also a new kind of musical instrument; John Healy and others create paintings of moving light; Rauschenberg causes his sculptured-paintings to speak, and John Cage composes a work called *4'33"*—in which the musicians 'perform' four minutes and thirty-three seconds of silence. In this work it is Cage's claim that the incidental sounds of creaking chairs, breathing, street noises, whispers become the music.

The greatest variety of experimentation in the theatre today is to be found in America. Its theatre is perhaps the most avant-garde in the world, and its two most important influences would appear to be Antonin Artaud and John Cage. One of the most tangible results of Artaud's influence is to be seen in the increasing concern with environmental theatre. Indeed this would seem to be the one recognizable concern of world theatre, from the work of Grotowski in Poland to the church operas of Benjamin Britten; Peter Brook's *Oedipus* at the National Theatre with the actors stationed all round the auditorium to Peter Schumann's Bread and Puppet Theatre in the streets of New York; all echoing the Russian experiments of Meyerhold in the 'twenties and of Okhlopkov in the 'thirties.

Now, however, complete environments are being created for productions. Allan Kaprow's *18 Happenings in 6 Parts* took place in three adjoining plastic-walled rooms, the spectators changing place in the interval. For Robert Whitman's *The American Moon* the spectators sat in six tunnels facing a central playing space. Jim Dine's *The Car Crash* enclosed the audience in a completely white environment. The performers also wore white and he even wanted the audience to be provided with white caps and smocks in order to integrate them with the space. In another work by Allan Kaprow, *A Spring Happening*, the standing audience watched through narrow slits in the side walls of a long 'box-car'.

The theatre is still largely rooted in the nineteenth century, with its tradition of an entertainment presented on a stage, framed by a proscenium arch, before serried ranks of people. Periodically designers and directors have tried to break with this convention but are thwarted by the archaic convention of flies and the other limitations of outmoded buildings, or else, as at the Chichester Festival Theatre, or the Round House in London, merely present proscenium arch productions in the round!

Indeed, whenever an attempt is made to break through architecturally—in England certainly—it is always, significantly, backwards in time to the apron stage of the Elizabethan playhouse or the Greek arena. Yet as we move towards the close of the twentieth century and man's arrival in space, where is the NEW theatre of the year 2001?

At the turn of this century, as we have seen, Gordon Craig dreamed of a stage where forms rose and fell in astonishing variety and seeming endlessness. In the 'thirties Artaud had a vision of a theatre which surrounded and embraced the audience who were to be caught up in the action.

For such a theatre what is required is a space which will provide the greatest physical and scenic flexibility, involving grids, hydraulic lifts, revolves, tracks, scrims, screens, domes, levels— and all able to be lit from above, beneath and every side.

The theatre must give the audience of today a new experience of space. It is as necessary for us to re-discover a relationship with space, the space around us, as it is to explore outer space. We need to experience afresh the height and depth and breadth of space, its intimacy and immensity.

John Cage, influenced by the *I-Ching Book of Changes*, has been chiefly responsible for the use of chance and indeterminacy in music, writing and theatre. Although we are all familiar with the use of improvisation in the theatre as a means of arriving at greater truth and spontaneity in performance, few will be so familiar with the term 'indeterminacy', which dictates the limits within which performers, in dance, music or drama, are free to choose alternative material provided by the choreographer, composer or director. Because the performers usually function independently and

K

do not respond to choices made by their fellow performers, there is none of the give-and-take that is found in improvisation.

Michael Kirby in his recent book, *The Art of Time*, describes *The Marrying Maiden*, a theatre work created by Jackson MacLow, one of Cage's students, in which characters and speeches were selected from the *I-Ching*. 'The order, duration of speeches, and the directions for rate, volume, inflection and manner of speaking were all independently ascribed to the material by chance techniques.'

When the work was presented in 1960 by The Living Theatre, although there was a basic blocking of the production by Judith Malina, other actions were inserted at random by the employment of a pack of twelve hundred cards, each one containing stage directions such as—'Scratch yourself; use any three objects in an action; kiss the nearest woman,' etc. These were given to the performers, in full view of the audience, by a stage-manager who rolled dice in order to determine the throw of the cards.

Of course much of what is happening in the arts in America to-day was anticipated, as we have seen, by the German Bauhaus and by the Dadaists. Tristan Tzara, for example, composed poems by shuffling a pack of cards, on each of which was inscribed a word, and drawing them at random from a top hat. Similarly Arp and Duchamp employed the rules of chance in their work.

The Living Theatre is often criticized because of the unevenness of its acting talents and skills, a certain rough unhewn quality. It is likely that they, in common with many other avant-garde groups, would claim that such criticism is mistakenly based upon traditional concepts. Just as any performance may be called 'music' which employs sound, and 'dance' which employs movement so, too, according to John Cage there should be no boundaries between art and life. Given such a premise, of course, technique no longer becomes necessary. The suspension of disbelief being no longer an ideal, the new theatre rejects all traditional techniques: story-line, naturalistic representation, plot, suspense, climax, dénouement. In the nineteenth century the ideal was a theatre larger than life. From the 'eighties onward the search was for a theatre that would be true to life. Now, as R. J. Schroeder points out in a brilliant analysis of the new underground theatre, the search is for a life-lived-now-theatre . . . 'the present generation has an almost paranoiac demand for fragmentation, discontinuity, multi-sensation. In rejecting narrative and form, all pretensions to art, it seeks to assault and directly involve the viewer.'

In their search for a greater immediacy and the breaking down of the barrier between audience and actors, many directors and choreographers prefer to work with untrained or non-dancers and non-actors, using simple, everyday movements that require no technique or skill, the performers merely being arranged in a sequence of completely alogical patterns. Since tour-de-force, virtuosity, skills and techniques are qualities no longer called for, it follows that anyone can be a dancer, an actor, a performer. The reasoning behind this theory is that since drama and dance were intended originally to be performed, not seen, what matters is the personal and individual experience of each participant, even though to the outsider it might seem as though nothing is happening. The fallacy of this theory is that both primitive and traditional societies were group-orientated, the actions of the individual reflecting and furthering the ends of the group. In addition we know that primitive societies show a degree of sophistication and skill that would startle many of the advocates of non-art as a return to the origins of drama!

Of course the increasing fragmentation of society today and the spectacular breakdown of traditional values, especially in America, is reflected in the arts. It is this vague yet specific feeling of disorientation that has led to an epidemic of non-theatre activities such as Happenings, Events and Activities. The latter, like children's games, are the acting out of situations—without limitations of time—often intentionally meaningless. In *An Anthology of Chance Operations*, Walter de Maria propounds a theory of 'meaningless work'. In discussing his approach to Activities (a name coined by Michael Kirby), he stresses the need to avoid a pleasurable activity—'lest pleasure becomes the purpose of the work'. He describes the procedure for his work, *Beach Crawl*, which involves the systematic placing and displacing of three stones. The final instruction is, 'Then shout as loud as you can, "Well, that's new, isn't it?" Then throw the three stones into the ocean.' In *Mirror* by Chieko Shiomi, the performer is instructed to stand on a beach, facing away from the sea, and while looking in a mirror, to walk backwards into the sea.

One of the most elaborate Activities, described in an issue of the Tulane Drama Review, was *Calling*, by Allan Kaprow, carried out in August 1965. Briefly, three people were stationed one Saturday afternoon on different street corners in New York. At a specified time separate cars picked them up. Each of the individuals was then covered from head to foot in tin-foil. The cars were then parked, each in a different spot, and the drivers departed, leaving behind them the human packages.

The process was repeated with three other individuals, each of whom was wrapped in muslin and tied with cord, and three other drivers. Finally, three of the packages were delivered to Grand Central Station and propped against the information booth. Each of the three human bundles then unwrapped himself, went to a telephone booth and dialled the number of one of the participants who had helped to drive or wrap them. For five minutes the three people in Grand Central Station and the three people in their three separate apartments throughout the city listened to the ringing. After each telephone had rung fifty times it was picked up. 'Hello.' The correct name was asked but the recipient of the call hung up without saying anything more. Saturday's part of *Calling*, all carried out to an exact time schedule over several hours, was complete. The following day an even more elaborate sequence concluded the whole operation.

Although, as Michael Kirby points out, no one saw all of the actions of which the piece was composed, each of the participants did experience the piece in its entirety. 'They were not only aware of their own actions and those of the other participants with whom they were directly involved, but they each read the script and had been briefed. They knew what was taking place in other parts of the city even though they could not be there, and this knowledge became part of the aesthetic experience.'

With such Activities theatre is being used as a means to enable people to enact private fantasies. In *Calling* the fantasy is that of its creator, Allan Kaprow, and the participants take part in it almost ritualistically. Ann Halprin, however, is more concerned with people acting out their own fantasies. With her Dancers' Workshop Company in San Francisco she has been experimenting with spontaneous unrehearsed sessions of up to fifty people—a cross-section of the community, ranging from students, architects and businessmen to psycho-therapists, tourists and hippies.

In the autumn of 1967 she conducted a series of experiments based upon the idea of myths, meant 'to evoke our long-buried and half-forgotten selves. Each evening will explore a different relationship between the audience and the performers, between our awareness, our bodies and our environments. The audience should not be bound by accustomed passivity, by static self-images or by restricted clothing. "Myths" are your myths. They are an experiment in mutual creation.'

Ann Halprin is interested in a theatre where everything is experienced for the first time. 'I have come back to the ritualistic beginnings of art,' she records, 'as a sharpened expression of life, extending every kind of perception. I want to participate in events of supreme authenticity, to involve people with their environment so that life is lived as a whole.'

Certain general conditions are first suggested to the group in an outer briefing room. Thereafter, anyone is free to participate or observe. Very soon, she noticed, people began to arrive regularly at these sessions to start their own improvisations as a warm-up. 'They know they won't be told what to do. They are going to do what they want, or make or allow to happen. People really like to have this kind of responsibility. It gives them a feeling of self-esteem, a chance to use their full capacities . . . Through group contemplation and discussion the evening can be transformed from a passing turn-on into art, a part of a person's being.'

When asked why she considers the public wants to determine its own artistic environment, she replies, 'We can no longer depend on our master minds. There is too much for one mind to master . . . It's wonderful to see what happens when you release people's resources . . . one person determining everything for everybody—it just can't be like that any more. It doesn't have to be like that.'

Typical of the various myths was that based on the image, *Carry*. For this people sat on high levels, all facing one another for a long time while drums rolled. Finally people were asked to volunteer to choose a person and carry him along the passage. This led to variations such as two people carrying one person; five people carrying two; five carrying one, and so on. Gradually the group became aware of the archetypal connotations of the act of carrying: the child carried in the womb; the bride across the threshold; the corpse to the grave; the Pope to the altar, etc.

In *Atonement*, after being briefed and deciding whether to participate in this 'ordeal', the audience entered the studio one at a time and stood facing the wall, looking into a blinding spotlight. The walls and floors of the studio were entirely covered with newspapers from one day's edition. Only one selected page was used, in complete repetition. They chose a position, altered their clothing, and remained still and silent for one hour. A loud continuous roll on a snare-drum was played in the centre of the room.

The participants afterwards returned to the briefing room and were asked to think of two words that best described their experience. They formed small groups and using these two words, shared their experiences.

'Perhaps in the future my rôle will need to be redefined,' reflects Ann Halprin. 'I am coming to see the artist in another light. He is no longer a solitary hero figure but rather a guide who works to evoke the art within us all. This is the true meaning of seminal theatre.'

Her words echo those of the English director, Joan Littlewood, who rejects the idea of the genius director. 'My belief,' she states, 'is in the genius of each person.' One of the most original and gifted directors and the first to create an ensemble in the English Theatre with her Theatre Workshop company, she has opted out of the present system, preferring to work informally, and therapeutically, with groups of young people, although she still dreams of 'a theatre not of actors but of artists'.

A unique phenomenon of the American scene is The Living

Theatre, a nomadic community of actors, their wives and children, led by Julian Beck and his wife Judith Malina. Numbering at the last count some forty souls, they have wandered through Europe—where for four years they were in exile from the tax man—and the United States, sharing everything in common. 'They are in search of a meaning in their lives,' observes Peter Brook, 'and in a sense even if there were no audience, they would still have to perform because the theatrical event is the climax and centre of their search . . . In The Living Theatre three needs become one: it exists for the sake of performing; it earns its living through performing; and its performances contain the most intense and intimate moments of its collective life.'

The irony is that while attacking the bourgeois capitalist system they still exist off and get their living from it. They have talked for a long time now about taking theatre into the streets, about the need to reach the economically under-privileged, something which The Bread and Puppet Theatre has been doing for the past eight years.

The Living Theatre regard traditional theatre as merely a salve for society, enabling the public to return in safety to its bourgeois way of life. 'We feel there is a need for change,' says Judith Malina. 'We feel that our whole culture needs to be changed. It has to grow away from what is destructive to what is creative. We have become over-intellectualized, divorced from our bodies, from real feeling. Even love, man's full potential, has become an abstraction.

'If we could once again become feelingful people and not shut ourselves off from one another, then we would not tolerate the injustices in the world. It is part of our process to try to unite mind with body, to heed those intimations within ourselves of immortality.'

Julian Beck takes up her argument. 'Words have become a barrier, an alibi,' he says. 'It is so easy to justify a war in words but if you are there on the battle-field, confronted with the appalling blood-shed and horror, how can you? We are not rejecting the use of a text in the theatre, so much as the use of words to create an alibi.'

Beck describes the company as a community in process of formation. 'It is important to reflect in our lives what we are trying to say on the stage. We are trying to solve our individual lives as a community.' Listening to them speak one is reminded of those communistic societies which flourished in America in the last century—the Harmonists, the Separatists of Zoar, the Oneida and Wallingford Perfectionists, the Shakers. It is very easy to imagine them, like the Amish Community today, being exempted from National Service and income tax—set apart.

Although pacifist by conviction in their personal lives, in the theatre they make a systematic and violent assault on the audience. In one of their most recent works, *Frankenstein* —a collage of Grand Guignol, shadow-play, Yoga, meditation, gymnastics, howls, grunts and groans—the effect upon the audience is like being present at the wedding in Belsen of Maria Marten and Sweeney Todd. As though in the Chamber of Horrors at Madame Tussaud's we see, on the various platforms erected within the outline of a human head, people being crucified, lynched, guillotined, buried alive, their hearts transplanted. What takes place on the stage is the representation of yesterday and today, riotings in the streets of Paris and Chicago: the monster that is created is our own bestiality let loose and out of control. The Living Theatre in holding up a mirror to nature reflects those restless, wild, daemonic energies that lie so lightly beneath the urban and urbane veneer of civilization. Audiences are compelled to recognize the truth in part of what is portrayed. An audience confronted by such daemonic energy is mesmerized. Audiences today are not accustomed to such a totality of performance in the theatre. We witness a community of actors driving themselves and sometimes us into a state of near trance or possession, sweat streaming down their naked bodies, froth flying from their mouths, as they blast their way through the conventions of nineteenth-century theatre. For four or five hours the audience is likely to be battered, bored, stimulated, provoked, assaulted. The shocks, assaults, noises, boredom get under the skin so that no one who has ever seen The Living Theatre is likely to forget the experience, while the re-iterated chants of Fuck for Peace, Free the Blacks, Abolish the Police, Abolish the State, Viva Anarchy, Fuck for Peace, are likely to stick, like hidden persuaders.

'If only we can make the spectator feel pain at a public ceremony,' says Beck, 'this may be the route by which we enable him to find the way back to his feelings, so that he will never want to commit violence again.' He likens a performance by the company to a church service conducted by actors. 'I don't know if this is a cleansing process,' he reflects, 'but I hope it may be relevant to the world now, and will drive people to change things. If people lived in really creative communities then they'd fight as hard for the success of that community. We are revolutionary anarchists and we are starting with ourselves. The struggle will always continue. It is the greatest gift given to us to participate in that creation.'

In the autumn of 1968 Judith Malina cried from the stage of the Brooklyn Academy in New York—'I demand everything— total love, an end to all forms of violence and cruelty such as money, hunger, prisons, people doing work they hate. We can have

tractors and food and joy. I demand it *now!*' At the end she and
Julian Beck led the audience out naked into the streets.

Again and again, it will be observed, the emphasis is upon feeling. Megan Terry, author of the play *Viet Rock*, declared, 'I want
my audience to feel rather than to think.' In 1968 she offered a
new play, *The People vs Ranchman*, in which Ranchman, an
accused rapist in police custody, is depicted dying in the gas-
chamber, the electric chair, on the gallows—and he goes on being
resurrected in order to join in the shouting and heckling with the
rest of the cast. As *Time Magazine* reported, the absence of
rational content was what was worth thinking about. 'It is not that
The People vs Ranchman is a bad play. It is not out to be a good
one in terms of drama's traditional concern with fate, foibles,
languages and ideas. Like the propaganda plays of guerilla theatre,
this play is intended to be a felt experience by the audience.'

As the audience found its way to its seats before the start of
Megan Terry's play, so it was hustled and barked at by the actors.
Tom O'Horgan, director of *Hair* and *Futz* and *Tom Paine*, says
that in trying to get rid of the fourth wall between the audience
and the actors he envisages in the theatre of the future 'lions under
one's seat'.

In the meantime, in the continuing search for greater together-
ness, clothes are shed by actors and audiences alike, while Yayoi
Kusama invites her audiences to join in a love-in. She has led
naked guerilla raids on the Statue of Liberty, Wall Street and
once, in Central Park, she set up a naked 'crucifixion' with two
youths having sex at the foot of the cross. Tom O'Horgan, in one
scene in *Tom Paine*—in which he wanted to emphasize the horror
of war—had the soldiers carried on strapped to poles, their pants
down, genitals exposed. It was in *Hair*, however, that he brought
nudity to its fullest, and most logical, exposure. Now he finds
nudity not enough and has been experimenting with 'naked' suits,
made of rubber, complete with sexual organs. Already the sex act
has been performed on the New York stage, albeit off-Broadway.
It is but a matter of time before mice, snakes, rats are let loose
among the audience; before the head of a real canary is chopped
off during a production of Strindberg's *Miss Julie*. Regularly in
New York one may witness at Destruction of Art sessions cockerels
being killed, violins and pianos smashed—Michael Kirby even
reports a violin being smashed on a man's head and blood pouring
down his face. Quite soon we shall see, as in William Golding's
Lord of the Flies, a ritual pig-killing, a mass orgy and finally—a
human sacrifice. The wheel will have turned full circle.

Half-baked and half-digested psychological theories abound,
make the headlines, become the vogue, make a reputation, even a
fortune. Yet the acting out of fantasies does not, alas, lead auto-

matically to psychic freedom. The ability to integrate on a psychological level requires certain disciplines and intelligence. It is a
scientific truth that only a few can respond to psychological
analysis. The Masters of Zen understood only too well that many
are called but few are chosen.

However, although in the new non-art preached and practised in
America there is much that is pretentious and even nonsensical,
it does seem that people like Ann Halprin and Peter Schumann
are reaching out towards the solution of a problem that is almost
entirely ignored by the theatrical profession. Within the thirty
remaining years of this century we shall experience a drastic
upheaval in our whole way of life. Shorter working and longer
leisure hours will mean an entirely new approach to the purpose
and function of the arts. It is not improbable that yet one more
barrier will be broken down—that between the professional and
the amateur. The thousands of unemployed actors will find themselves diverted to other forms of creative activity, not necessarily
in the arts, and acting will no longer be a profession. Theatre will
no longer be an entertainment for a minority relaxing at the end
of a day's work, but a meaningful activity for thousands of
leisured people. The importance, or the meaning, of Joan Littlewood's withdrawal from the English theatre in order to work
with young people, has largely been ignored. I think it probable
that we shall see the drama, the dance, taken out of the hands of
the professional and restored to the people. This is the true meaning
of the Activities, Happenings and Events that I have described in
this chapter—the participation by ordinary people in rites of
their own making.

Such a situation will make certain artists more important to a
community.

'I am coming to see the artist in another light. He is no longer
a solitary hero figure, but rather a guide who works to evoke the
art within us all.' Here, surely, Ann Halprin sees the true and
lasting place of the artist in society. Ordinary people, faced with
increasing leisure time, will not be content with a continual fantasy life—that way lies infantilism and retreat from life. It is
through the exercise of disciplines and skills that people grow in
an understanding of life and of art. A perfect performance of a
raga in Indian music has been likened to a marriage between artistic calculations and human impulses. The artist is one who has
acquired such disciplines over many years and become a Master.
He is like the primitive magician, the medicine man or the shaman
who is 'not only a sick man; he is, above all, a sick man who has
been cured, who has succeeded in curing himself'.

It is the Masters who must teach and each community will have
need of a Master or Masters. The artist of the future will have to

come to recognize more and more his rôle as teacher. Many today are aware of this, artists such as Yehudi Menuhin, Martha Graham, Jerzy Grotowski, Alwin Nikolais, Peter Schumann, E. M. Forster. The purpose of theatre, as of all art, must still be to cross our frontiers, exceed our limitations, fill our emptiness— fulfil ourselves.

Maurice Bowra, writing about primitive song and ritual, has observed,

Above all, it is an art and does what art always does for those who practise it with passion and devotion. It enables them to absorb experience with their whole natures, and thereby to fulfil a want which is fully satisfied neither by action nor by thought. In the end, like all true art, it enhances the desire and strengthens the capacity to live.

It seems to me that the last thing the actor does today is to absorb experience with his whole nature. He is a professional paid to entertain by means of certain skills, which are often quite minimal, but—except in the case of the true artist—his real life is elsewhere. And the audience knows this. Unless theatre becomes more profoundly meaningful, as much a way of life as a way of work, work involving the whole of an actor's being, stretching him to his fullest, then the theatre as a profession will die. This may be inevitable. It may even be necessary.

Jerzy Grotowski believes that a renewal in the theatre can only come 'from people who are dissatisfied with conditions in the normal theatre and who take it on themselves to create poor theatres with few actors'. Certainly now more than ever there is a need to take time out for re-assembly. There is a need for more centres, like Grotowski's Laboratory Theatre in Wroclaw, where small companies may search and research. This has been the inspiration for Stage Two, the new workshop and centre for research, based in London, which is a major extension of the Hampstead Theatre Club.

Stanislavsky, half a century ago, realized that 'for the new art new actors are necessary, actors of a new sort with an altogether new technique'. There is no art that does not demand virtuosity, and such a company of actors requires what may be called 'guaranteed' time in which no one is working towards a deadline. To work slowly as is necessary, from the ground up, under the guidance of experienced teachers, without financial complications, and reasonably insulated from the hysterics of the competitive field, such a project, such a laboratory, should be the first concern of every country, every state, as it is in Poland today.

Bibliography

Chapter 1

Lommel, Andreas *The World of the Early Hunters* Evelyn, Adams & Mackay, London 1967

Wain, John *Sprightly Running* Macmillan, London 1962

Chapter 2

Komisarjevsky, Theodore *Myself and the Theatre* E. P. Dutton & Co., New York 1930

Slonim, Marc *Russian Theatre* Methuen, London 1963; World Publishing Co., Cleveland 1961

Stanislavsky, Constantin *An Actor Prepares* Bles, London 1937; Theatre Arts, Inc., New York 1936

Stanislavsky, Constantin *My Life in Art* Bles, London; Little Brown & Co., New York 1924

Tynan, Kenneth *Tynan on Theatre* Penguin Books, London 1964 (first published as *Curtains* by Longmans, Green, London and Atheneum Publishers, New York 1961)

Chapter 3

Cole, Toby & Chinoy, H. K. *Directors on Directing* Vision & P. Owen, London; Bobbs-Merrill, Indianapolis 1964

Fishman, Morris *Play Production: Methods and Practice* Herbert Jenkins, London 1965

Gyseghem, André van *The Theatre in Soviet Russia 1943* Faber, London 1943

Hartnoll, P. (ed) *The Oxford Companion to the Theatre* OUP 1967

Marshall, Norman *The Producer and the Play* Macdonald, London 1957

Moore, Sonia *The Stanislavski System* Gollancz, London; The Viking Press, New York 1966

Roslavleva, Natalia *Era of the Russian Ballet (1770–1965)* Gollancz, London 1966

Stanislavsky, Constantin *My Life in Art* Bles, London; Little Brown & Co., New York 1924

Taylor, J. R. *The Penguin Dictionary of the Theatre* Penguin Books, London 1966

Chapter 4

Slonim, Marc *Russian Theatre* Methuen, London 1963; World Publishing Co., Cleveland 1961

Chapter 6

Guthrie, Tyrone *A Life in the Theatre* Hamish Hamilton, London 1960; McGraw-Hill, New York 1959

Moore, Sonia *The Stanislavski System* Gollancz, London; The Viking Press, New York 1966

Chapter 7

Cole, Toby & Chinoy, H. K. *Directors on Directing* Vision & P. Owen, London; Bobbs-Merrill, Indianapolis 1964

Craig, Edward *Gordon Craig: The Story of his Life* Gollancz, London; Knopf, New York 1968

Goffin, P. *Stage Lighting for Amateurs* J. G. Miller, London 1955

Hartnoll, P. (ed) *The Oxford Companion to the Theatre* OUP 1967
Marshall, Norman *The Producer and the Play* Macdonald, London 1957
Simonson, Lee *The Stage is Set* Dover Publications, New York 1932
Stanislavsky, Constantin *An Actor Prepares* Bles, London 1937; Theatre
    Arts, Inc., New York 1936

Chapter 8

Bowers, Faubion *Japanese Theatre* P. Owen, London; Hill & Wang, New
    York 1959
Marshall, Norman *The Producer and the Play* Macdonald, London 1957
Saint-Denis, Michel *Theatre: The Rediscovery of Style* Heinemann, London;
    Theatre Arts Books, New York 1960

Chapter 9

Cole, Toby & Chinoy, H. K. *Directors on Directing* Vision & P. Owen,
    London; Bobbs-Merrill, Indianapolis 1964
Marowitz, Charles (ed) *The Encore Reader*, Methuen, London 1965

Chapter 10

Artaud, Antonin *The Theatre and Its Double* Grove Press, New York 1958
Coast, John *Dancing out of Bali* Faber, London 1954
Gyseghem, André van *The Theatre in Soviet Russia 1943* Faber, London
    1943
Stanislavsky, Constantin *My Life in Art* Bles, London; Little Brown & Co.,
    New York 1924

Chapter 11

Grotowski, Jerzy *Towards a Poor Theatre* Odin Teatrets Forlag, Denmark
    1968; Methuen, London; Simon & Schuster, New York 1969
Magriel, Paul (ed) *Chronicles of the American Dance* Henry Holt, New York
    1948

Chapter 12

Magriel, Paul (ed) *Chronicles of the American Dance* Henry Holt, New York
    1948

Chapter 14

Bowra, Maurice *Primitive Song* Weidenfeld & Nicolson, London; New
    American Library (Mentor Books) 1968
Brook, Peter *The Empty Space* MacGibbon & Kee, London 1968
Eliade, Mircea *Shamanism* Routledge, London; Princeton University Press
    1964
Kirby, Michael *The Art of Time* E. P. Dutton, New York 1969
Schroeder, R. J. *The New Underground Theatre* Bantam Books, London
    1968

Acknowledgments

I should like to thank my friend Mrs Emma Dickinson but for whom this book could not have been written; Mrs Foster of the British Drama League for her enthusiastic cooperation; Mrs Jane Nicholas of the British Council; Mr Horace Judson of *Time Magazine*; Mrs Rosemary Cole, Mrs Ethel Issler, Lady Diana Cooper and Mr Chris Bazeley.

The extracts from *My Life in Art* by Constantin Stanislavsky are reprinted with permission of Geoffrey Bles Ltd, London. American edition copyright, 1924, by Little Brown & Co; copyright, 1948, by Elizabeth Reynolds Hapgood; copyright renewed, 1952. The extracts from *An Actor Prepares* by Constantin Stanislavsky are reprinted with permission of Geoffrey Bles, London. American edition copyright, 1936, by Theatre Arts, Inc; copyright, 1948, by Elizabeth Reynolds Hapgood; copyright renewed, 1964.

The extracts from *The Theatre in Soviet Russia 1943* by André van Gyseghem are reprinted by permission of the author and Faber & Faber.

The extracts from *The Producer and the Play* by Norman Marshall are reprinted with permission of Macdonald & Co. Ltd.

Extracts from *Curtains* by Kenneth Tynan. Copyright © 1961 Kenneth Tynan. Reprinted by permission of Atheneum Publishers and the Longman Group Limited.

The extracts from *The Stanislavski System* by Sonia Moore are reprinted by permission of Victor Gollancz Ltd and The Viking Press, Inc.

Illustrations nos. 12, 17, 18, 19, 20, 21, 22, which originally appeared in *Towards a Poor Theatre* by Jerzy Grotowski are reprinted by permission of Odin Teatrets Forlag and Jerzy Grotowski.

Illustrations 2, 3 and 11 are reproduced from *Theatre Arts Monthly* September 1936. Copyright, 1936, by Theatre Arts, Inc. Illustrations 5, 6 and 7 are reproduced from *Theatre Arts Monthly* August 1932. Copyright, 1932, by Theatre Arts, Inc. Reprinted with permission of the Appia Foundation, Berne, Switzerland.

General index

Numbers in italics refer to illustration plates

Plays and other works